The SAP Consultant Handbook

Your Sourcebook to Lasting Success in an SAP Consulting Career

Updated SAP Consulting Info:

For the latest information on the SAP consulting market, and to read Jon Reed's analysis of SAP career trends in the NetWeaver era, turn to the very end of this book. There, you will find details on how to access Jon Reed's free SAP career information online - much of which is created specifically for those who purchased the *SAP Consultant Handbook*.

Also by Michael Doane

SAP Blue Book, A Concise Business Guide to the World of SAP (Jon Reed, Contributor)

Also by Jon Reed

Resumes from Hell
(samples available on www.resumesfromhell.com)

About *Resumes from Hell:*

Some resumes are good, some are bad, and some are simply from Hell. The all-too-real resumes in this book were no doubt written with the best of intentions, but a job search can be a misadventure. A wacky resume is a sure-fire way to derail your job application and slip from the interview pile into the "joke file." In this illustrated "how not to," former recruiters Jon Reed and Rachel Meyers open up their own joke files, and share highlights from the worst (and funniest) resumes they ever received. From "Questionable References" to "Hostile Email Interactions," Jon and Rachel take the reader through more resume mishaps and job search meltdowns than they ever knew existed, sneaking in a bit of job search wisdom on the fly. The resumes in this book have been changed to protect the not-so-innocent, but *Resumes from Hell* is proof that truth is still stranger – and funnier – than fiction.

The SAP Consultant Handbook

Your Sourcebook to Lasting Success in an SAP Consulting Career

JON REED & MICHAEL DOANE

This book was written by Jon Reed & Michael Doane.

"SAP" is a registered trademark of SAP Aktien-gesellschaft, Systems, Applications and Products in Data Processing, Neurottstrasse 16 69190 Walldorf, Germany. The publisher gratefully acknowledges SAP's kind permission to use its trademark in this publication. SAP AG is not the publisher of the book and is not responsible for it under any aspect of press law.

Published by eCruiting Alternatives, Inc.

Printed in the United States

ISBN 0-9725988-0-4

Original Edition Published in March 1999

Updated September 2004

Cover Design by Rachel Meyers

Machiavelli offers the advice that only a wise prince can be wisely advised.

SAP consultants are not offering advice to princes. They are performing a service in a field of business and princes (or princesses, for that matter) will not be numerous or visible.

Let us forget that the term consultant can mean 'advisor'. Think of a successful SAP consultant as one who offers equal amounts of time, sweat, expertise, and passion to an endeavor that will usually have an enlightened end, but in the day-to-day will not always make perfect sense.

Only the time is billable. The rest is the raw material of a career.

Dedications

Jon Reed would like to dedicate this book to Rachel Meyers, who has shown the entrepreneurial grit that marks success in careers SAP and otherwise, and to his colleagues at SAPtips, who are a constant reminder that with the right team, you can take on just about anyone.

Michael Doane extends a salute to Graham Davis, a globe-trotting SAP of many years, and to his children, Sarah and Guillaume, who know firsthand how SAP means Suitcase and Passport.

CONTENTS

Part III: Managing Your SAP Career

Consulting Rates: Ebb and Flow 116

Enhancing Your Market Value 134

When to Hold 'Em, When to Fold 'Em 151

Balancing and Measuring Multiple Offers 159

The Finer Points of SAP Contracting................................ 165

Preface (with Jon Reed's 2004 update)

Jon Reed's update, September 2004: Greetings to all you aspiring (and current) SAP professionals! When Michael Doane and I first issued this book in 1999, we had no idea it would become the industry standard for those seeking to break into SAP and those who are seeking to remain the most marketable SAP consultants out there. We appreciate your continued interest in our book and in the SAP field.

Although the SAP field has changed dramatically in the last five years, there's no question that there are still a lot of great careers in SAP for those who are committed to SAP and to professional excellence. In recent years, I have continued to publish an extensive amount of information on SAP career trends, much of which has been specifically geared for the readers of this book. I have also launched an SAP publication of my own, called SAPtips (www.SAPtips.com), which may be of great interest to those of you looking for deeper technical and functional SAP know-how.

Recent readers have convinced me that this book's secrets of consulting success and SAP fundamentals are timeless. However, there is also a need for updated market information. The best way to approach your SAP career is to read this book first, honing in on the sections that round out your SAP or consulting knowledge. Then, proceed to the end of the book, where you can learn where to find the latest information I've published on SAP career trends.

Eventually, I'll publish a companion volume to this handbook, but in the meantime, if you start with this book and combine it with the new material I've issued online, you should be well prepared to get the most out of the SAP market. I have seen thousands of SAP careers unfold over the last decade, and while I can't promise anyone success in such a competitive market, I can assure you that those consultants who have put the principles of self-education and skills enhancement espoused in this book into action have continued to thrive. SAP is

always re-inventing itself, so doesn't it make perfect sense that those
who succeed in SAP should do the same?

With NetWeaver just getting off the ground, and the install base of
SAP customers fully committed to SAP, I think there's at least a
decade of rewarding SAP work to come for those who are savvy
enough to spot an opening that suits their skills and interests. I wish
you all the best of luck in your SAP career pursuits. Now, on with the
original preface. -JR-

To anyone totally new to the subject of SAP, this book will not make
perfect sense. Our intent is to provide career guidance, not explain
the ever-widening, ever-deepening world of SAP and its expanding
list of products and services. Such an effort has been undertaken
elsewhere and we advise newbies to read the *SAP Blue Book, A Concise
Business Guide to the World of SAP* prior to delving into this tome.

SAP R/3 is a complete suite of integrated business applications and
the firm, SAP AG, continues to expand and enhance its offering at an
alarming and disarming rate. As such, consulting opportunities vary
from the highly technical to the highly strategic and virtually
everywhere in between. The SAP arena includes all business functions
and all businesses, from healthcare to manufacturing to utilities,
public sector, media, retail, aerospace and defense, consumer
packaged goods, oil and gas, automotive, communications, and much
more. Further, success in SAP consulting will, over the long haul,
require parallel knowledge of SAP and one industry focus. Until 1998,
SAP R/3 was the shoe meant to fit every foot. Now that shoe has
been tailored to allow for any kind of dancing, from waltz to tango to
conga line.

Our basic intent is to provide the first ever sourcebook for people
who are already in the fields of SAP consulting as well as those who
think they would like to break in. As the implementation market
contracts, the rest of the market is continually expanding (mid-market

firms, front office, supply chain, strategic information sub-systems, and much more). For over five years, SAP has held between 28% and 33% of the worldwide ERP market and we expect this predominance to continue. As such, there are opportunities galore and we hope to enlighten you to the "best practices" (while apologizing for the term) to apply in your SAP career navigation.

The authors are grateful to a number of people who have contributed to this book, including Betty Costa, Mike West, Patti Walsh, Rob Doane, George Zatulovsky, Scott Gilbert, and a number of colleagues at Grant Thornton and Allen Davis & Associates.

Part I:

Opportunity and the SAP Consulting Market

Who Are You? What Do You Want?

Consulting Supply & Demand: A Gap Analysis

The Seven Deadly Myths of the SAP Job Market

Who Are You? What Do You Want?

All it takes is a week or two in the lush, rampant, and sometimes weedy fields of SAP recruiting to understand that loads of people want to be SAP consultants and a majority of the candidates present themselves for one solid, scintillating, undeniable reason: money.

There are deep fields of SAP green out there, six figures as far as the eye can see. The admixture of a massive consulting shortfall and the feverish growth of SAP have lead to persistent billing rates in excess of $150 per hour. Many of the consultants have gathered these fees through competence and diligence. Many others have proven to be quick-buck artists playing hit-and-run. Even more have slipped somewhere between honorable and, well, less honorable, between competent and, well, compost.

Are you a college student striving for a BS in Computer Sciences and wondering which way to turn once the goatskin is in your palm?

Are you in a firm that has struggled to implement SAP and you have observed that a number of the consultants around you (six figures tattooed to their foreheads) know less about the subject than you do?

Are you an experienced, savvy software engineer with x years of C++, some serious background in networks, and a rage for code?

Are you a consultant with ten years of industry experience (retail, telecom, utilities, oil & gas), with a nice mix of project background?

Do you have a taste for room service, Spectravision, flight delays, shuttle buses, early morning wake-up calls, sudden challenges, off-the-cuff advice, paratrooper moments, and the will to keep track of hundreds of tiny pieces of paper (receipts) that are worth, by the foot, about $12,000?

Are you married? Do you have young children? Do you garden? Do you live far from an airport? Have you mastered the QWERTY keyboard?

Every single question in the above section cuts ice. Stop right here if you have bought a ticket for the long green and do not have this in return: Passion. Hard to measure and harder still to define.

If the passion we are speaking of were easy to define, this would be a paragraph, or a white paper. It will take the entire book to define it.

For example, if you garden, you may not make it as an SAP consultant. The travel involved often means that those geraniums will not get watered. Another consideration: young children need more than water and if you are gone from Mon to Fri, what's it all about? If you are the C++ programmer with a rage for code, you might find a position in an SAP techno-peripheral company, but you will not be a roving big bucks consultant. If you have not yet mastered the QWERTY keyboard, other horses will outrun you daily.

And you who are in a firm that is implementing or has implemented SAP, consider this for one full minute: could you replicate your performance if you a) parachuted into a company that you do not know and b) have a limited amount of time to accomplish feats that you have only accomplished once before?

At this writing, here is what SAP consultants make:

Partner (Big Five)	something criminal
Partner (standard firm)	$200K-$400K
Project Manager	$120K-$200K
Senior Consultant	$100K-$160K
Consultant	$ 75K-$150K
Flunky	$ 60K-whatever falls out of the sky.

Let us assume that you have a soul and only aspire to become at best the partner in a standard firm. This book will teach you what it takes to do so. And whether or not you garden, and whether or not you can type 'Cat' in fifteen seconds or less, we will guide you through the C and the A so that you can rap down that T all by your lonesome.

But before we go a step further, another raft of questions:

Do you care about improving the lives of those around you?

Does it matter to you how you spend your work time or is it only a paycheck?

Is it sacrifice or teamwork?

Are you in for a five-year run or a quick fix?

Are you a hound or a terrier?

This last question is a touch subjective, but only a touch. Terriers annoy. They bark way too much. And in the world of SAP consulting, terriers have their place. In basement C. Hounds move more smoothly, last longer, and get there with less noise. Our advice: be a beagle. Show your eyes and not your vocal cords. Listen up. Soak. Prosper.

In your SAP working life, if you last 10 years, you will log more hours than you will spend with your family in twice that time. Assume that 46 weeks of the year are spent at work. If you are thinking that you get less than 6 weeks of vacation, consider long weekends, training time, sick time, etc. and you will find yourself in this chart all the same.

Hours	Weeks	Years	Total
40	46	10	18400
45	46	10	20700
50	46	10	23000

Assume you are on the high end of the hours per week scale and you can see that you will spend 23,000 hours in the SAP fields. How you spend those hours is important, we agree, but how you frame those hours, how you lay the foundation for how you will spend those hours, and what you will get from those hours, is partly the subject of this book. Will it be time well spent, or will those be like hours in a dentist's chair?

A Vision of the Model SAP Consultant

At a writing seminar we once attended was a special panel discussion on the question, 'How does one get a first book published?' Questions were posed about the value of agents and editors, whether or not carbon copy submissions were acceptable, whether manuscripts should be double or single-spaced...all the minutiae of book submissions. The members of the panel did their best to address each of these questions, but one finally blurted: "The best way to get published is to write a REALLY good book."

By the same token, we are often asked what it takes to succeed in SAP consulting. Is it vital to know ABAP? Is training worthwhile? Which modules have the greatest market? Should I go Big Five or consider the smaller firms?

So, again, let us cut to the chase: the best way to succeed in SAP consulting is to be a REALLY good consultant.

We will address all of those other issues in the remainder of this book, but first we feel it necessary to lay down some rail as to what a really good SAP consultant is. Try this:

> A professional with clear-eyed business knowledge, (what it's all about), a knack for teaching (no one succeeds in a vacuum), and twin senses of urgency (keeping the project moving ahead) and empathy (hey, these are people here).
>
> Oh, and solid knowledge of SAP R/3.

We are making a point here about the order of importance. It is true that solid knowledge of SAP R/3 (pick your module) is sufficient to get you through the front door of most projects. It is also true that if that SAP knowledge is all you have in your kit bag, you will revisit that door sooner than you think.

Consultants are mercenaries who parachute into a client world, rapidly gather information about the terrain, execute to a plan, and depart, seldom to return. What they leave in their wake is rarely as clear as 'success' or 'failure'. Some leave their knowledge behind, having shared it with the client body. Others have helped the client bring a fuzzy vision into focus and then into reality with R/3 as the enabling systems support.

Others have merely 'clicked' out some R/3 configurations according to business process designs, then headed off into a murky sunset and another assignment for cash.

Baby sitters are paid by the hour, just like consultants. Think about what kind of baby sitters you had as a kid. One just sat in the front the TV and yelled at you to be quiet. Another made you popcorn and sat you in front of the TV while she chatted on the phone. Yet another made you popcorn, turned off the TV, and read a book to you. But the best one, *the best one*, taught you how to make popcorn, showed you how to turn off the TV, and then taught you to read your very favorite story.

With only SAP R/3 skills, a consultant is more like the babysitter who can make popcorn, dial a phone, and manipulate the remote control of a television.

When it comes to consultants, the best ones learn what story a client wants to learn and makes certain that, before the end of the project, the client knows how to read that story and live it out.

Business knowledge first. Consulting skills second. SAP skills third. All three required.

Consulting Supply & Demand: A Gap Analysis

The Shortfall of SAP Consultants

In mid 1998, there were approximately 320 firms claiming to have SAP consulting activities or practices in North America. More than 3,000 firms had licensed SAP, and the demand for skilled consultants to support their implementations was estimated at more than 20,000.

The shortfall is estimated as anywhere from 3,000 to 8,000 consultants. One reason the estimates vary is that the definition of 'skilled SAP consultant' is not universally agreed upon. If we only include people with a rich mix of industry experience *plus* SAP training and experience, *plus* consulting background, there are probably only about 5,000. If we simply look for people who have received training in SAP and have one year or more of experience, the total number rises to around 15,000.

One thing is certain: the market for good SAP consultants will last for a relatively long time. This is the answer that precedes one of the most FAQ, namely "How long is this SAP market going to last?"

Later in this book, we will analyze and forecast trends because sectors of the SAP consulting market will flatten out, others will emerge, and still others will be transformed. But go back to the pronouncement and note the basic qualifier: *good* SAP consultants. Right now the market for even poor SAP consultants is still fairly warm, but it is cooling rapidly. Such consultants are still tolerated in the Fortune 500 circles (where they can hide behind numbers of other consultants), but not in the small and middle-sized markets where their weaknesses are quickly exposed.

Still, a shortfall of 20% to 30% to the demand for SAP consultants will not be bridged by the year 2000, nor even by 2002 unless…

1. the North American economy experiences a downturn and,
2. without the Y2K problems, fewer firms are looking to change their IT supports, so
3. SAP licensing lags, and
4. new and existing competitors chip away at SAP's 30% share on the client server market.

This could happen, but we are betting that it will not and so should you. Bear each of these possibilities in mind and balance them with…

1. R/3 Version 4 fits the middle-sized market need for industry specific compatibility, and
2. Fortune 500 firms that have already implemented core modules turn to more sophisticated fare like Plant Maintenance, Workflow, Internet capacity, and the like, and
3. R/3 Version 4 lures the high end automotive industry out of its wait-and-see stance of the past five years, then
4. General Motors accelerates its implementation schedule.

Perhaps that 'great big sucking sound' that Ross Perot warned us about will be just this: General Motors needing 10,000 consultants to help it implement SAP worldwide.

If this second scenario unfolds, even the lousy SAP consultants may well survive into the next millennium. But don't count on it.

The Origins of the Shortfall

In the 1980's SAP AG made great strides throughout Europe, South Africa, and Australia with its R/2 mainframe-based offering. R/2 never caught on in North America. In 1992, SAP America had $180 million in revenues and was barely on the ERP radar. By the end of 1992, there were less than 300 experienced R/2 consultants on the continent. In 1993, the unexpected and overwhelming popularity of R/3 created the gap that we are still trying to fill in 1998.

Since 1993, the majority of implementation projects have been understaffed, not only in numbers of consultants but more especially in terms of the quality of the consulting. SAP clients have had to pay high rates for relatively unqualified help and their backlash was evident in the American press by mid 1995. The 'high cost of SAP' was widely echoed as was the notion that SAP implementations take an eternity. By the end of 1996, SAP was clearly on the defensive. Yet through this same period, licensing continued at a wild pace (90 per month in North America) and few clients cancelled their implementations.

In 1997, SAP America hit the $1.6B mark. That is a climb and a half from the $180M of 1992 and is indicative, all by itself, of the rampant market for SAP consultants. During this period, no one needed a book like this one to make money in SAP consulting. All that was required was some background in SAP R/2 or R/3.

Filling the Gap, with Honor

We have already seen a gold rush to fill the gap of SAP consulting and by the time the ink is dry on this page, another twenty pretenders will have signed on to another implementation project. Of these twenty, five will be banished within five months for lack of competence, another five will have jumped to a greener glen, and two more will be dropped because the scope of the project will come into focus and their skills will not be needed. Of the remaining eight, a team will be formed. Work will advance. Clients will be enlightened. And the team will be two or three members short and hours will be stretched. This is where those $150 per hour are worth it. Are you worth it? And how much of that $150 will land in your pocket?

As for the five who dropped out for lack of the proper skills, read on. And for the five who quickly moved on to greener pastures, we will probably see you again. And for the two who slipped through the cracks because the scope shifted, hey, that's showbiz. Dust yourselves off, and let us carry on. There will remain new ballparks for you to play in.

One of the greatest impediments to filling the gap is the paucity of decent SAP training. On newsgroups and bulletin boards, 5% to 10% of the postings are queries about training and the answers are seldom satisfactory for anyone other than ABAPers.

Another impediment to filling the gap is the worldwide shortage of information technology resources. The high octane North American economy, combined with a fifteen-year drag in IT grads from American universities, has opened windows of opportunity in dozens of domains, from client/server to Internet industries. The worldwide shortage of qualified professionals is vast and wide and the bottom line is that we are in a sellers' market when it comes to recruits. The SAP consultant shortage is only the most publicized; similar shortfalls exist in dozens of other business-technical and information-related fields.

Andersen Consulting reported a 35% attrition rate for 1997 and that seems to be the rate for most consulting firms. To understand the import of such high attrition, consider the table on the next page.

A firm that begins a year with 100 consultants and recruits an additional 100 per year will have only 253 consultants in its cupboard at the end of a four-year period.

Year	Jan	Recruits	Losses	Dec
1	100	100	-35	165
2	165	100	-58	207
3	207	100	-73	235
4	235	100	-82	253

Clearly, the burden is on firms to find you, develop your skills (i.e. billing potential), and keep you. How you capitalize on this market will depend largely on how you behave once you are in it. Mercenaries can go on riding this wave for a while longer; professionals can ride it for years to come.

The Seven Deadly Myths of the SAP Job Market

SAP is the Elvis Presley of the ERP software world. It is popular, well-publicized, fat, attracts followers, sells like hotcakes, and inspires more myth and rumor than can ever be waded through. (BaaN, by comparison, is John Denver. It is rumored that K-Tel will be offering cassette versions on late-night television).

In this chapter, we explore and debunk a number of myths about SAP consulting that have sprung up, clouding the vision of wannabe consultants and diverting some career paths into bewildering side streets.

Myth #1: If You Are Willing to Lower Your Contract Rates, You Can Break into the SAP Market

The second half of this myths goes "…and after a year or so you will have the necessary experience to get full rate."

This is simply not true. Technical contractors have historically been able to lower their rates to gain consideration in hot skill areas. In the Fortune 1000 arena, clients are making multi-million dollar investments in SAP and are prepared to pay whatever it takes, albeit within reason, to hit implementation deadlines on time. Getting contractors with proven SAP experience is much more important than getting a bargain rate on contractors.

In the small and mid-sized market, ditto and then some. For these markets, project teams are often built with a 'one-of-each' point of view: -one consultant for financials (FI/CO), another for logistics (SD/MM), etc. A rookie with a lower rate would be a very weak link in the chain and therefore unacceptable.

We know of a prospective recruit who volunteered to work in nuclear sites or other dangerous locations to gain experience. Another offered his services on a sliding scale from $20 an hour to $100 an hour over five months provided he got on-the-job training throughout. A spreadsheet exercise reveals that this candidate would be paid $48,000 over five months *while learning to do the job.*

Month	1	2	3	4	5	Total
Rate	20	40	60	80	100	
Hours	160	160	160	160	160	
Pay	$ 3,200	$ 6,400	$ 9,600	$12,800	$16,000	$48,000

Nice try.

The reality is that firms no longer hire just anybody with SAP background or others who might fit in time. Instead, they will pay top dollar for teams that can meet budgets and deadlines and will sometimes wait for those teams to come free rather than rush to fill a project roster with leftovers.

Myth #2: Relevant Experience in Other Enterprise Software Greases the Rails into SAP Consulting

There are numerous enterprise software programs in competition with SAP, but experience in a different program does not mean a smooth transition into SAP. The best way to get into SAP is still to be in the right place at the right time, on staff at a company that has decided to implement. The next best way is to get on board a consulting firm with an SAP practice and work your way onto it. It is this second route that sometimes allows a Peoplesoft consultant to get cross-trained in SAP, or vice versa.

Mid-sized to large consulting firms offer the best route into SAP for those who have skills in other packaged applications. Cross-training is simpler than new training and cheaper as well. Further, if you have a solid track record as a consultant, these firms will look more favorably on your candidacy. Then again, if you already have that track record (be it in Peoplesoft, BaaN, or Oracle) why would you switch?

Note: there is not yet the glimmer of a market for "enterprise software" consultants who have hands-on skills in several of the major programs. At this time, it is simply too much technical territory to cover. But perhaps in the future, there may be a new breed of "enterprise software consultants." For now, the only real use for cross-application expertise is in pre-sales, and even then broad knowledge of functionality differences between programs is more important than hands-on technical mastery.

Myth #3: Big Five Firms Do Not Pay a Competitive Salary; the Best Route is Straight into Contracting

Here is a scenario that is played out countless times:

Bill Graysuit, with one year of SAP background and two years of industry experience, is recruited into a Big Five firm for $80K a year. Bill is pleased with this contract and eagerly heads off to his first implementation assignment.

During the second week of Bill's engagement, he finds himself sharing lunch with two independent contractors who have been brought in to flesh out the Big Five team. Over shrimp salads and bottled water, he discovers that the contractors are each making $110 an hour. Before he can dislodge the shrimp that is stuck in his gullet, Bill learns that his Big Five firm is billing $150 an hour for his services.

Shrimp salad looks funny when stuck to the ceiling. And Bill looks kind of silly as he drives home on a mostly-empty stomach, growling now with angry juices.

What Bill has not taken into account:

1.   Those contractors almost certainly have wider and deeper experience than Bill in terms of industry, SAP, and consulting.

2.   His $80K represents a first-year salary. The Big Five offers a career path, prestige, etc. etc. etc. and the rubber on Bill's professional tires is barely worn.

3.   The economics of the deal. How much has Bill's firm spent training him? How much down time will he have during a calendar year? What will the firm spend on company events, internal training, methodologies, sales, and all the rest?

4.   Bill's risk tolerance. Is he truly ready to sit on a nice, cozy chair in his make-shift home office and wait for a call back on the next round of resumes he sent out (while wondering to himself if he has enough SAP skills to make it as an independent contractor)?

Several points have to be made here. First of all, it is the client who might best be outraged at a $150 per hour price tag for Bill's services. One year of industry plus one year of SAP plus zero years of consulting have probably not geared Bill for that kind of price tag. Secondly, Bill is gaining very valuable experience, which he will later be able to use as a springboard to bigger bucks within his firm, or with another, or as an independent contractor.

In general, it *is* true that Big Five firms are not paying as much as other firms, and for good reason. The vast majority of Big Five clients are in the Fortune 500 group and the project teams run from twenty to two hundred consultants. The Big Five firms tend to assign a combination of vets and rookies, with the rookies clearly being the "high margin" pieces to the puzzle. But how did those vets become vets?

Indeed, this knowledge is often a motivating factor when SAP consultants decide to leave the Big Five and move into contracting. And it is also true that there are plenty of smaller consulting firms prepared to pay much more than the Big Five for the same level of SAP experience. The Big Five ARE generally paying better than end-user permanent positions, but that's about it.

Having said all this, we do think that skipping a Big Five position to go straight into contracting is not necessarily a good idea. Contractors with Big Five experience routinely edge out the competition for contract assignments. Like it or not, companies hiring independents place a high value on Big Five credentials. A stint in the Big Five can do a consultant's resume a world of good. Further, a vast number of successful small consulting firms were founded by, you guessed it, ex-Big Five consultants. So if your goal is to become a high-end contractor, small consulting firm founder, or to advance into an SAP project manager, do not rule out the Big Five. Beyond the prestige of a Big Five firm, there is training, diversity of experience, and a visible career path. Some people never leave the Big Five; they become (take a breath) partners.

Myth #4: If You Have the SAP Skills, Companies Will Fly You In from Around the World to Work in the U.S.

Our e-mails and newsgroups are filled with queries that relate to this myth and we pray that the message will go out:. at one time this was the case, but not anymore.

From 1992-1996, the shortage of experienced R/3 consultants led firms to import help from Germany, Australia, Holland, and South Africa, and the results were mixed, to say the least. Experience in SAP R/2 did not always translate to consulting skills with SAP R/3 in the North American environment. Many of the candidates who came across the waters had loads of in-house SAP experience and were useless in the implementation fields. And many more were simply panning gold and their job performances left a lot to be desired.

By 1997, the glitter of foreign consultants began to fade, and has continued to fade as more and more North Americans enter the market.

This is most telling for ABAP personnel. The ABAP glut continues and worsens as more and more people see ABAP as a port of entry to both SAP and the United States. It may be true that such people can find $40 to $60 an hour (not too shabby) as contract ABAPers but this leads to a sub-myth: ABAP is an integral part of an SAP installation. See the next myth.

There is a continuing market for good SAP consultants, whether they come from Germany, Australia, India, or Mars. But the gold rush years, during which anyone with real SAP experience could call the tune, is over. Over. *Over.*

Some of the logo partners (Big 5, Cap Gemini, IBM et al) will still fly people in for interviews in the U.S., but this is the exception, not the rule. One of the problems is simply the unpredictable delays in visa processing. Only the largest consulting firms are willing to wait for an unspecified time until the visa is done. Smaller consulting firms and companies, with specific project deadlines, simply cannot wait. They cannot hire ahead of the sales curve as can the larger firms. And hiring officials worry that while a visa is pending, another offer or situation can come along. The moral of the story: for those of you who plan on working in the U.S. for a long time, a company that will process your green card might even be worth a cut in salary.

Myth #5: ABAP Programming Is an Integral Part of an SAP Installation

Coding is not programming. Programming is not software engineering. And SAP R/3 is not software.

The assumption that many people have is that ABAP programming is an important and lasting part of an SAP installation. This assumption is unfortunately shared by candidates, clients, and far too many SAP consulting firms.

Let us examine a few rock-hard facts:

1. SAP R/3 is configurable, table-driven software. As such, it can be implemented and maintained by business people, with the peripheral support of techies.

2. ABAP coding should be limited to parts of R/3 that are labeled as "user-exits". Any changes to the R/3 code outside of these areas will require system maintenance as the R/3 installation evolves, either through new configuring or SAP upgrades.

3. ABAP programming is needed for interfacing. Interfacing is counter to the principles of R/3. The firms that continue to retain legacy systems usually fail with their R/3 endeavors. ABAP interfacers have a short career-span.

It is not hard to learn how to code in ABAP. Coding is of little value to most firms with SAP R/3. What is useful is a software engineer with some industry knowledge and some background in one or more SAP modules. These are the ABAP folks who will have careers rather than temporary gigs.

Those ABAP programmers who commit themselves to developing the latest and greatest SAP connectivity solutions could be in good shape, however. An aggressive focus on "hot skills" areas that bridge the gap between companies, suppliers and customers will serve ABAP programmers very well.

Myth #6: SAP Training Courses are a Great Conduit for Breaking into the Market

Supplementary technical training never hurts an IS career, but there are no guarantees. And not all training courses are created equal. Certifications from SAP America carry more weight than other private training courses. Those in permanent jobs should research carefully before leaving a job to take an SAP training course. Contractors should realize that it is not easy to go straight from SAP training into SAP contractor. A "pit stop" at a Big Five or similar firm that will round out your training is a better bet, and even Big Five firms are reluctant to hire SAP trained applicants without real experience. Even a so-called "hands-on" training course or prototype work is not considered a guarantee in this current hiring market.

Certifications from SAP America are certainly useful, but are rarely an absolute requirement for most positions. Perhaps 5% of all job orders require certification, but on the other hand at least 75% of hiring officials will consider certification as an asset, just as long as the applicant also has SAP work experience.

The bottom line: if you have money to invest in training and do not have to leave a permanent job to do it, go ahead and give it a shot, but otherwise, use caution.

Myth #7: True SAP Experts Don't Have to Fit in with the Team

Only the best SAP "hired guns" can afford to be aloof while they are on projects. There are a few consultants who have ten to fifteen years of SAP, including R/2, and these may be the only consultants who do not have to answer to anybody as long as they can perform.

There is, for example, a legendary consultant of German origin who now hails from Arizona. This man is proficient in half a dozen modules, speaks four languages, and has lectured extensively. His daily fee is around $5000. You are not him.

In a tight job market with an increasing emphasis on knowledge transfer, the consultant who can not only implement the system, but who can also bring in-house employees up to speed, is the consultant who is in demand.

As technology becomes the essential tool that corporations rely on to streamline business processes, the time of the 'techie' who does not have to interact with broader groups is over. SAP professionals may have hot skills, but the most successful pay attention to the 'soft' communication skills involved in project management, training, team-building and knowledge transfer. And by the way, these skills also make a major difference during the interview and hiring process. Without rapport (another 'soft' skill), there is no hire.

Part II:

ng Fields and Battlefields

SAP Consulting Models

There are four main options for SAP employ as an SAP consultant:

1. SAP independent contractor
2. Permanent consulting positions with small or mid-sized consulting firms
3. Permanent consulting positions with Big Five and other large consulting firms
4. Permanent positions (internal consulting) with end-user companies.

Of course, there are countless other employment options, such as contracting through a small or large consulting firm, or taking on a temp-to-perm position. There is also a wealth of possibility in the many firms which are technology partners of SAP. However, we are concentrating on SAP consulting only.

Independent Contractor

An independent contractor in SAP will typically be hired directly by companies, although being hired as a contractor through a consulting firm is another possible option.

Advantages: Being paid hourly by the company eliminates any middle-person, providing you with the best possible profit margin for yourself. You will be able to secure far better rates contracting this way than through any kind of permanent position. For the entrepreneurial-minded, this may be the ideal arrangement. You negotiate your own projects and you will always know what kind of margin you are billing out at.

Disadvantages: Negotiating your own rates and marketing your own services can be a challenge. If you are being paid as an independent contractor, and not as a W-2 contractor (which is another option that may be feasible) you will be responsible for making your own tax payments, securing your own health insurance, etc. Incorporation can potentially help you to protect yourself from the tax liabilities of being an independent contractor, but this requires additional start-up expenditures and legal costs.

Verdict: A great option for the seasoned veteran with an independent streak and a desire for an excellent rate. Not always a great option for those with less SAP experience. If you want to focus primarily on your SAP work and don't want to deal with the logistics of building your own business, this option may not be for you.

Note: a later chapter covers this model in far greater detail. Read on.

Permanent Employment in a Small or Mid-sized Consulting Firm

Mid-sized Consulting Firms

With the opening of the mid-sized market (which includes firms with $200M to $2.5B in annual revenues), there is far more opportunity than ever before for mid-sized consulting firms. The clientele is out of the financial and geographic range of the Big Five and the market itself is wide open, including literally thousands of prospective clients.

These firms are broken into three categories:

1. Longstanding firms which have opened SAP practices
2. Smaller firms which have acquired another smaller firm
3. Smaller firms which have succeeded in the recruit & retain arena.

The first category includes firms like Grant Thornton and Arthur Andersen, to name the most prominent. These firms have management consulting practices in areas besides SAP, in addition to their traditional activities of audit and tax. Employment with such firms bespeaks of permanence and stability and careers paths can be horizontal (i.e. from one practice to another) as well as vertical (i.e. from consultant to partner.) Such firms also offer a national presence, making re-location less of an issue.

> **A Larger Playing Field**
>
> Whereas the Big Five are usually fighting over the Fortune 1000 clients, small and mid-sized firms have a much larger playing field.
>
> CIC Research, an independent research firm based in San Diego, defines the middle market as organizations with revenues of $50 to $500 million.
>
> According to International Data Corporation (IDC), there are 27,032 organizations in the United States within this revenue range.

The second category of mid-sized SAP firms is more difficult to assess. Companies that are built by acquisition often have tenuous cultures and hard-to-define identities. Such firms often have relatively high rates of attrition as the merger of disparate firms results in some disillusionment on the part of the acquired firm's consulting force. Of the three categories, this is the most perilous and least attractive if you are looking for a 'home'.

The third category of mid-sized SAP firms offers more stability than the second category but less dimension than the first. Identity is not an issue in that these firms have established themselves in the marketplace and their growth is usually derived from a combination of excellent client service and a respectful company culture.

Smaller Consulting Firms

Since 1995, literally hundreds of such firms have sprung into existence with an annual drop-out rate of around 33%. If you try a Yahoo search on "SAP Consulting", you will find most of them and once you have entered their web-sites, you will be faced with a mixture of fact and fiction.

Most of these firms have 15 to 25 W-2 employee consultants but tend to claim a larger roster. The 'gain' is usually attributed to a second roster of independent contractors who are aligned to the firm in one way or another. Often, these same contractors are also listed for other firms. The point is, the core of the firm in question will be those 15 to 20 W-2 consultants.

Smaller firms can afford to pay higher salaries than Big Five firms. A favorite tactic small firms use to lure SAP consultants is to increase the salaries of their employees while underbidding Big Five firms to obtain contracts. The theory here is that a smaller profit margin per hour is better than none, and smaller firms typically have less overhead than do the larger firms.

Small firms figure if they can pay you better, you will reciprocate with your loyalty. Of course, some small firms are start-up or undercapitalized and will have less money to offer than their bigger competition. Besides the potential for big dollar salaries, the best smaller firms offer a friendly, more personal atmosphere and the potential to grow with the company into leadership positions.

On the down side, however:

Some small firms may be shady operations with unethical employment practices. The boom in SAP consulting that started in 1993 gave rise to a gold rush and many of the firms that sprang up in subsequent years were no different than panhandling firms with high phone bills and cool web sites.

It is important to research small firms carefully. Some are outstanding, but some may not adhere to their agreements once you begin your employment. Be wary of all promises regarding bonuses, vacation, and time on the road that are not specifically documented in writing. An additional disadvantage to smaller firms is that the client base may be less diverse. If a small firm loses a client in San Francisco, there may be no other West Coast clients and you might find yourself working on the other side of the country from your home base. In addition, smaller firms may not have the resources and systems to provide thorough training and complete benefits packages, and they definitely do not have the same resume prestige/name recognition factor as some Big Five firms do.

In the same light, these firms undergo massive changes faster than do the larger firms. New partners are brought in, clients are found or lost, one partner has a life crisis, another hires his incompetent wife as director of HR...the terrain changes from quarter to quarter and the consultant in the field gets little or no news of what's happening on the home front.

Verdict: If you want good money with more job security than a contract and are willing to travel extensively, take a look at some quality small firms. When we say 'take a look', we mean a *looong* look. Be prepared to weather change and to keep your antenna up especially while you are in the field. Look twice at offers of partnership after x months in the fold, and be sure that your ongoing SAP training budget remains intact.

Permanent Employment in a Big Five or Large Consulting Firm

Advantages: Although the reputation and status of these large firms varies, they will generally add a prestige factor to your employment history. Their benefits packages are typically comprehensive, and their bigger client base makes it more likely that you will be able to stay closer to your region of choice, although this much is rarely guaranteed, no matter what the size of the firm.

Larger firms are better equipped to provide you with training and help you to make career transitions to other hot client/server- based consulting opportunities. A tour of duty in a large firm can also be very valuable for anyone who eventually wants to start their own consulting firm or work as an independent consultant in the future.

Another significant advantage offered by larger firms is the possibility of advancing into a full 'Partner,' or equity position. Some SAP consultants really do want to take on the challenge of leaving hands-on work and moving into project management, practice supervision, and ultimately a partner-level position.

Disadvantages: To some, particularly those with family commitments, the high travel typically expected by a Big Five firm is a drawback. Although salary offers vary widely between firms, these larger firms do not typically pay as well as the previously discussed options. The prestige factor of these firms, and thus their advantage to you on a resume, also varies considerably from firm to firm. The internal reputation of the larger firms as employers also varies depending on who you talk to. In a large firm, there is a greater likelihood of feeling like a cog in a large corporate machine. Another danger is the possibility of seeing your initiative and advancement squelched by crusty layers of management.

Verdict: Great for those SAP professionals who place a premium on long-term job security and professional training and development. A good way to pick up broad implementation experience before heading into a management role or starting out on your own. Not always a great option for those with immediate financial considerations or those who like freedom and autonomy. Large firms vary widely in pay and philosophy. Do your research.

Permanent Employment at an SAP End-user

Advantages: Permanent employment at end-user companies has several major perks. A key strong point is less travel. For those with family and relationship commitments, this is a priceless advantage, one that can rarely be measured in dollars and cents.

An implementing end-user can be one of the best work environments, with less employee turnover and a great team environment. Lasting friendships may seem like a subjective thing to consider as a plus, but end-user companies can be like a tonic to the SAP road warrior. Further, in such an environment, you get to see a project through to the end and beyond.

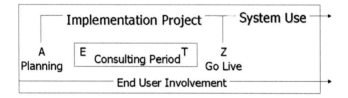

Consultants rarely have the opportunity of seeing the fruits of their labors. End-users usually do, and often have a far better understanding of post-implementation issues.

Some end-user firms offer attractive stock option plans, which make the modest salaries a bit more attractive. For those consultants who are strongly committed to building an impressive net worth but who do not want to travel, companies with aggressive stock options programs are worth considering.

Disadvantages: Very few end-user companies are in the financial position to compete with SAP consulting salaries. Indeed, they do not generally try to, as these companies believe that consultants are paid more precisely because of the challenges of being on the road. If you are considering a low travel position, do not be insulted by a lateral salary offer, or even one that offers a bit less than what you are currently making. Your main paycheck is the quality of life.

Of course, if you are single and/or free of family commitments and do not mind traveling, then the end-users' typically lower salaries may not be so appealing. Another major disadvantage to an end-user SAP position is finding yourself in a company in turmoil. An SAP implementation usually engenders a high level of change (and stress). Nothing is more claustrophobic than a permanent position in an unstable company. Research end-user companies very carefully.

Verdict: Great for those who do not want the road life and want to appreciate the fine times with family and friends. Also a good chance to hook into a growing company in an industry you have a long-term stake in. Not always a good option for those who like the travel and want big money and lots of different SAP projects. Excellent for those who want to focus on one key project, assuming the company is a blue chipper.

Conclusion

It is always wise to carefully review and prioritize these employment options early in your job search. Typically, you will make the best short-term career decisions after you have written down your long-term professional and personal goals. Then you will be better able to assess which of these employment options will best facilitate your own long-term agenda. It is important to remember that you must create your own approach, which may be very different depending on whether or not you have a family, whether or not you want to be in a management position or own your own company, etc.

No matter which option you pursue, there is no substitute for careful research. Every company and opportunity is different. You must take it upon yourself to learn which companies have the best reputations. Talk to your co-workers, obtain annual reports. Compare and evaluate.

When Size Matters: the Big Five

From Big Eight to Big Six to High Five

Once upon a time there was Ernst. Ernst was a lonely accountant who wanted more clients, more money, more moreness. Another accountant, Whinney, also wanted more, so it only made sense when Ernst and Whinney tied the knot. For a while, Ernst & Whinney were happy. They shared clients, created tax and consulting operations, and made new partners; life was good. But after a while, Ernst and Whinney looked around and saw they were not the biggest family on the block. It was a tough call turning polygamist, but finally they took the plunge and married that handsome Arthur Young. Somehow, Whinney got shoved aside when they were changing the gold leaf on the office doors, and Ernst & Young is how we refer to the firm today.

Following the genealogy of Big Five firms is not easy. Years ago, of course, they were referred to as the Big Eight. These were Price Waterhouse, Coopers & Lybrand, Peat, Marwick & Mitchell, Deloitte,

Haskins & Sells, Touche Ross, Ernst & Whinney, Arthur Andersen, and Arthur Young.

Coopers married Lybrand. Deloitte married Haskins and Sells. Then Touche & Ross married in, but there was a stretch in the U.K. when Deloitte, Haskins, & Sells were married to Coopers and Lybrand, but that marriage didn't last longer than that of Julia Roberts and Lyle Lovett. Peat married Marwick and we have already covered the family history of Ernst (& Whinney) & Young. The begetting and begatting seem endless and soon enough, if history takes its course, it will simply be The Big One.

A variety of mergers took place in the late 1980s, reducing the number from eight to six and more recent mergers have again confused the issue, so we are living with a Big Four, or is it Five, or is it the "High Five"?

All of these firms, whatever their marriages, have followed the same evolution. First, they were audit firms, banking on Anglo-Saxon legislation that requires independent financial audits (reviews, check-ups) of all firms. This practice, known today as "assurance" was for years the bedrock of these firms.

Second came "tax" as the audit firms found that clients needed professional advice. And with the rise in importance of information technology and parallel evolution in business practice, each of the original "Big Eight" firms opened Management Consulting practices. SAP consulting in each is a separate "consulting practice".

Since this book is dedicated to SAP consultants, we feel compelled to include other firms within this same subject, by virtue of their similarities in size and market share:

Andersen Consulting – only the largest consulting firm in the world.

CSC – only the second largest consulting firm in the world.

IBM – semper magna, semper aqua.

Consider the following table:

$US Consulting Revenues (millions)

		1997
1	Andersen Consulting	2863
2	CSC	2000
3	Ernst & Young	1798
4	Deloitte-ICS	1500
5	Coopers & Lybrand	1270
6	KPMG	1066
7	Price Waterhouse	806
8	IBM	570

Source: Kennedy Information Research Group

It looks as if we have reached to get back to a Big Eight, but with the recent merger of Coopers and Lybrand, there are really now seven firms that we are addressing here as PriceWaterhouse Coopers dukes CSC for the number two spot. Just for the sake of clarity, we refer to this crowd as the Big Five all the same.

How the Big Five Dominated the Mid 90s SAP Market

Given the lack of experienced SAP consultants in North America during the 'early' years of R/3 (1993-1996), Fortune 500 firms had nowhere to turn except to the Big Five (plus two) firms for SAP consulting assistance. The client attitude was "we've got a big job to do, with big software, so we need a big consulting partner." What they got were big problems, big bills, and some very big disappointments. The Big Five firms quite simply did not have experienced consultants in sufficient numbers to satisfy the demand. Rather than turning down the business, they shipped trainees (often straight from university or right out of client settings) through six-week SAP consulting academies in Dallas and Boston and then flooded Fortune 500 projects with these 'certified' consultants.

Further, these firms used implementation methodologies that were far better suited to IS implementations (including system development) than to SAP R/3. The result was that consultants were wasting time on tasks that were not required. The resulting implementation mess (high costs, long project duration) gave SAP itself a very black eye and the shiner is still visible.

Some Fortune 500 companies played gin rummy with these firms, shifting them in and out, replacing one with another, always in search of a winning hand. All the same, the Big Five continued to dominate the market because, as they say in this business, *no one was ever fired for choosing the Big Five.*

Another factor of Big Five predominance is the audit card. It is appalling to realize that Big Five firms with audit responsibilities for Fortune 500 firms are also given lead consultancy on SAP implementations. The obvious conflict of interest should negate such a combo, but back-scratching and cronyism often have more to do with contracting than do competence and integrity.

Back to that phrase "no one was ever fired for choosing the Big Five." In fairness, Fortune 500 firms find themselves in need of dozens, often hundreds, of SAP consultants for a given endeavor. No SAP consulting firm in North America has such numbers and clients are looking for single source consulting. They already have the software supplier (SAP), a platform partner (HP or IBM or Compaq or Sun), and they seek to keep the number of outside interlopers to a manageable few. Dial 1 B I G S I X seems to be the solution.

However, **none** of the Fortune 500 projects (either completed or still going) have been staffed by a single Big Five firm. All such projects inevitably required a patchwork team composed of Big Five consultants (often more than one) and 'resource augmentation' afforded by a multiple of the smaller firms. In such cases, one of the

Big Five firms has held the 'project lead'. Project management, methods, and (most importantly) resource planning are largely controlled by the project lead.

The Coca Cola Bottling Company (they hate it when you refer to the company as 'Coke') observed this amongst its Fortune 500 brethren and was determined to avoid the consulting mess it had seen elsewhere. The initial tack at TCCBC was to consign all consulting to Ernst & Young only. (Trick question: what firm does TCCBC's audit?) The project started in 1997. It is called the Infinity Project.

Big Five Opportunities and Shifting SAP Sands

Until 1997, the idea of going to a Big Five firm was almost a "no-brainer" for most SAP professionals who were considering a consulting career. The classic approach was to come off of an SAP end-user site and hop on board a Big Five firm for a year or two, and then jump a couple more times in the next year in search of the best salary and position. This "jumping-bean" approach is no longer viable.

Accelerated SAP

In brief, this is the now common method for implementing SAP R/3. It consists of five steps (referred to as the Road Map):

        1.   Project Preparation
        2.   Business Blueprint
        3.   Realization
        4.   Final Preparation
        5.   Go Live & Support

When ASAP came available in 1996, implementations began to accelerate and the success of the method (and its accelerating tools) is unquestioned. It should be noted that the large firms still use their own methodologies, often to the detriment of project success.

Up until 1997, the Fortune 500 projects dominated the SAP consulting scene. The Accelerated SAP methodology was still in its earliest infancy (see box), and most of the Fortune 500 projects were large and being served by Big Five accounts. There was a lot of budgetary latitude on many of these accounts, what some have called the "honeymoon" era in SAP. This honeymoon era gave an opening to very junior people, many of them college graduates, to jump in on projects and gain consulting experience.

The landscape has shifted considerably. There are still some larger projects on the horizon, and there will be more huge projects if SAP's industry solutions, such as IS-Retail, take hold and penetrate new vertical markets, but there is a greater level of fiscal responsibility and accountability on all SAP project sites. Big Five firms, typically using the classic "Business Process Re-engineering" approach, with SAP as the tool, are being asked to justify the sophisticated-sounding methodology and to keep "scope creep" under control. The key phrase now is "knowledge transfer." Do the work, teach the client how to do the work, and get out.

Further, SAP America has made a major effort to open up the mid-sized market. At first, it seemed that Big Five firms were going to ignore the mid-market and stay focused on larger projects, but now we are seeing these firms start to form mid-market groups and divisions. However successful these mid-market groups turn out to be, the Big Five will face serious competition when bidding on these smaller projects, especially when they are faced with a streamlined, no frills, no reengineering approach that many smaller firms have successfully adopted.

Those of you with a year or less SAP experience may still find your consulting options limited only to Big Five firms and a couple others. This is not because non-Big Five firms cannot train you; in fact, many of them now have very sophisticated training programs. The main obstacle is one of depth of experience. Smaller firms need you to be able to pull your weight soon after you are hired. They can train on top of what you have, but you will have to be responsible for a broad functional range on these smaller projects.

For example, we have seen end-users come off of very large projects where they have gained a year and a half of serious configuration experience, but limited to only a small part of a module, such as FI-AR. These backgrounds are generally too specific to be useful for a smaller firm, where you might be the only FI person on a project, but a Big Five firm can still utilize your background on other big projects where more specialization is possible and larger FI teams are in place.

But let's assume that you do have a broad enough range of implementation experience to consider a variety of consulting firms. Is the Big Five still a viable career path? The answer is a qualified yes. It all comes down to your professionals goals, and whether or not you are, at heart, a "big company/prestige" person, or an entrepreneurial person.

Two Paths to Follow

The change in the IT workplace demands that all of us see ourselves, to some degree, as entrepreneurs, prepared to make pro-active job changes to make sure our career stays on track. We believe there are two distinct profile preferences: the organizational person, and the entrepreneurial person. The organizational person tends to view him/herself in terms of pride and prestige with the organization. The entrepreneur tends to think of him/herself more as a "company of one," always reserving the right to move on, or come up with a new, innovative approach to the market. Whether you see yourself leaning towards one extreme or the other may help you decide on the type of consulting firms you should consider.

As a general rule, we have found that the **entrepreneurial types** are happiest in smaller firms, where performance can be recognized and rewarded more quickly. Also, some of the finest smaller firms are being run by ex-Big Five consultants (refugees, as it were) from an environment where performance often becomes the sideline to careerism. The bottom line is that you can utilize your Big Five experience to serve a variety of purposes. What is important is that you are conscious of your goals as you enter these larger organizations. Otherwise, you may get lost in the shuffle.

There are still two main strategies to be employed when joining a Big Five firm. One is the **"tour of duty"** strategy. This strategy is pursued by those who take a Big Five job with the intent of staying a few years, just long enough to gain some experience, some contacts, and that Big Five medal on the resume. The position is a stepping stone to starting a smaller firm, returning to a higher-level industry position, or heading into independent contracting. And there is no question that the "prestige factor" is the main positive ingredient that is common to almost all Big Five positions.

Name recognition still means something to many clients. We have noticed, for example, that contractors with a Big Five background seem to rise to the top of the heap when independents are being hired. Prestige is irrational, in that it does not mean that you are a more competent consultant, but it is a benchmark that has been used by more hiring officials than we'd care to mention. This prestige factor is more significant to those who are coming from smaller, lesser-known implementations. If you already have a prestigious MBA degree, or if you are coming off a major implementation site like Amoco or Intel, then the prestige factor is derived from the client in question.

The other strategy employed by some who join a Big Five firm is the "long term career," or **"partner track"** strategy. This track is for ambitious folks who see themselves as being compatible with the Big Five lifestyle and are prepared to climb (and claw) all the way to Partner. Although the path does get narrower at the top (and more than a few ambitious folks we know have been disillusioned by the games they have to play to stay on the partner track) there is no question that a partner-track position can be a very rewarding career end for some SAP consultants. For these people, SAP becomes a lever that "greases the wheels" of the partner track, making it an easier climb and one that keeps skills on the cutting edge.

This partner-track approach does require a willingness to travel over a longer period, and more importantly, a commitment to give "whatever it takes" for a number of years in order to get there.

Some people thrive in a Big Five environment and others wilt away, worn down by the size, impersonality (perceived or real) and circuitous career path of large organizations. These 'refugees' from the Big Five contribute to the flow of negative word of mouth about the Big Five that is not always warranted.

Partner

Senior Manager

Manager

Senior Consultant

Consultant

Consultant Trainee

When you become a consultant with one of these firms, you are given a vision of a career path that could, if you play your cards right, lead to a partnership. Being a partner means that you are an owner and thus participate in company strategy and profits. It is something like having tenure and this level of job security is alluring to many people. One consequence of having partnership as the goal is having to deal with the in-house politics that tend to surround consulting activity. Credit for 'success' becomes a slippery subject and 'failure' is a hot potato passed from hand to hand until *somebody* takes the burn.

Further, the team concept is forever put to the test when it comes to documents. Imagine you are a project manager who's been asked to put together the data for a proposal of services. Another group of consultants helps draft the proposal and together you create a solid plan, budget, and supporting documents. One partner reviews the proposal and changes some of the activities. Another partner reviews the revised proposal and rewrites the executive summary. If the client in question is already an audit client, then the audit partner chips in.

After running this track, your proposal of services scarcely resembles the document that you put together to start with.

What you may find after starting the project is that serving the client often takes a back seat to billing levels. A project manager is too seldom judged according to budget and timeline performance and too often judged according to how much extra work was sold to the client in the course of the project. Although this billing element is not an across-the-board characteristic of Big Five consulting, it is pervasive enough to bear this caution. Many of the Big Five refugees leave the arena just as they have risen high enough in the ranks to have to put up with this nonsense. Project work was great; selling projects less so.

Life Expectancy in a Changing Culture

One myth we would like to debunk right now is the myth that "you go to a Big Five firm for the superior SAP training." The SAP market has evolved significantly, and now there are a number of medium-sized firms, partnered with SAP America, that offer the same quality of training and certification that the Big Five can provide, sometimes better. The better of the smaller firms are able to focus on your individual needs and plan accordingly.

Some people go with a Big Five firm to provide them with stability "in case SAP bites the dust." We doubt that this is really a valid reason to go with a bigger firm. SAP is not going away any time soon, and when it does it will be a gradual process. We think that smaller firms may actually be nimbler in response to the changing market, and large-scale layoffs, if they ever were to happen to SAP consultants, might actually be more likely in a larger firm

One advantage we still see is a greater potential for cross-training, and dramatic career retooling. It should be obvious that a Big Five firm, with such a broad management and IT consulting practice, would be a better fit with those who are looking to make radical changes in skills down the line. Big Five firms also provide, as a rule, better "general consulting" skills training than smaller firms. Although most skills are best honed through use, we know many consultants who have liked the general training of some of these firms.

Of course, the obvious question you are waiting for is "which Big Five firms are the best for SAP," and "how do they differ from each other?" We are going not going to characterize better or worse amongst them, but we can point out a few differences.

First of all, not all Big Five firms play SAP with the same fervor. In essence, the order of billing magnitude appears to be:

> Andersen Consulting*
> PriceWaterhouseCoopers**
> Deloitte-ICS
> Ernst & Young
> KPMG

* Though part of the same boisterous family, Andersen Consulting must be distinguished from the firm from which it was derived, namely Arthur Andersen, which is now dwarfed by its elephantine child.

**What is interesting here is that prior to its merger with PW, C&L had maintained only a "window-dressing" U.S. SAP practice (to quote a C&L partner). We have heard a rumor that C&L will now create a "mid-market" SAP practice. We hear a lot of things and this rumor should be left on the "we'll see about that" shelf.

As a rule, we advise you to put the industry gossip aside and explore the option individually. All of these firms are reputable, and have similarities in terms of the prestige factor and the way the experience will look on your resume.

It is not enough to judge a firm based on word-of-mouth, particularly when you are dealing with firms of such size. Too often, a consulting firm is condemned because it sent a poorly trained consultant out on a company site or because one particular project was poorly handled. Anecdotal information does not provide an accurate reflection of this firm's conduct as a whole.

Further, many Big Five consulting firms have enough regional autonomy that you must assess them differently depending on the area of the country you are considering, or even the country itself. (As mentioned above, Coopers & Lybrand once maintained a minimum "window dressing" SAP practice in North America, while being a major SAP player in Europe and Australia.) For each firm, you may not be dealing with one reputation, but several, from several different locations, lumped together as rumors are passed along.

At the same time, the practices are different, and the cultures are different. We have seen people find legitimate opportunities in all five. In truth, these firms are always changing leadership, at least on the regional level, and your experience may differ dramatically depending on which region you will be working for. The only thing you can do is to keep an open mind and judge the "best fit" for yourself. None of these firms can hurt your career, but jumping on board one of them because you heard it was "the best" could be a mistake.

More times than not, we see that this "most comfortable fit" is more important than salaries, which tend to be similar anyway (and not as big as you can find outside of the Big Five). Many times we have seen a consultant turn down more money from one Big Five firm, only to go with one that seemed more comfortable to them personally.

Finally, you will find a few Big Five positions that do not involve travel. This can be great for those who want the consulting experience but do not want to be road warriors. These situations are a distinct minority, but they are out there. Sometimes they come in the form of "competency center" positions, other times they are long term engagements on one project. As a general rule, however, the Big Five have the same high-travel pros and cons as the smaller firms.

Conclusion

There is no firm that is objectively better than all the others. In their marketing, they all tout their experience, and all possess centuries of it. They all have major successes and glaring failures in their archives. They all expand and retract according to economic fluctuations.

Research your options carefully and look further ahead than your potential first year in any such firm. Go beyond hearsay by speaking to current employees of the firm in question, and check out their on-line information, annual reports, and other documents that give you a flavor for each firm. As you verify rumors and research the facts and figures, remember to consider several different variables: the firm's reputation amongst its employees, the firm's reputation with high-profile clients, number of consultants on staff, management structure, and opportunity for advancement.

At the same time, you should keep in mind that job satisfaction is a personal matter, not fodder for a glossy brochure. If you can, do some exploratory interviews with any Big Five firms you are considering and hear them out, "try it on." Often, negative opinions you may have heard are based on personality conflicts that would not necessarily speak to your experience with that same company. One Big Five firm is sometimes perceived as "too small," not as established, with a less impressive client base. But for another person, this firm has been perceived as "just right", still small enough to welcome an entrepreneurial mindset and advance people quickly. Interestingly enough, sometimes the firms that have the best reputations with clients may have the worst record with their own employees, or vice versa. Weigh out the total package in accordance with your personal priorities.

If you are wondering how the different firms breakdown in terms of total SAP consultants, the following figures from ComputerWorld may be of use to you. Hewlett Packard and IBM Consulting, though not officially "Big Five," are also included.

Total number of SAP consultants worldwide:

Anderson Consulting	3,000
IBM	1,500
Price Waterhouse	1,150
ICS, Deloitte and Touche	1,000
Coopers and Lybrand	665
Ernst and Young	660
Hewlett-Packard	320
KPMG Peat Marwick	320

Source: ComputerWorld, 1998

How to Get Your Start in SAP Consulting

The Most FAQ of SAP

SAP is still a rewarding and challenging field, but it is becoming maddeningly difficult to break into, even if you have relevant industry experience. To make matters more frustrating, there are few places you can turn to for guidance and information as you try to "break in" (of course, this book is changing all that for the better). To add insult to the general lack of information, most recruiters will not even return your call until you have at least a year's experience in the SAP field. Further, the "Big Five/Fortune 500" market is slowing down and the domestic U.S. market focus has shifted into the middle-market range, so the demand for junior level consultants is going down by the day, making entry into the field that much more of a challenge.

You can still get into this field, but it is going to take persistence and savvy and maybe even, God forbid, a touch of modesty when that entry-level SAP salary doesn't exactly blow you away. So if you are in pursuit of your first SAP position, you are out there on your own. You are going to need a good strategy and a strong commitment to self-marketing.

We wrote this book because we believe that there are many people who can make a real contribution to the SAP field, if only they can get their first project experience. We hope that you take our advice to heart, and use it successfully to break into this field and leave your stamp on it.

"I don't have any experience in SAP, how do I get involved?"

This may be the most frequently asked question of today's IS professional. The most important thing to realize, without allowing discouragement to set in, is that you are not the only one asking this question. There are thousands of people with strong technical, manufacturing, and financial backgrounds who are all trying to get involved in SAP in some way. You must find a way to stand out from this pack.

Before your resume is tossed onto a pile of dusty rejects, you should ask yourself some careful questions and come up with a plan. First of all, do you really want to be in SAP? Are you genuinely fascinated by what SAP does, or are you just breathlessly aware of the high salaries SAP professionals command?

No one knows how long the SAP market is going to last. At some point, the amount of people with SAP experience will reach a threshold and demand will level off somewhat, as will salaries. Whether this happens in the next two years, or three, or ten, it is all the same inevitable.

Before you put money and time into acquiring expertise in SAP, think seriously about your current skill set and its future. For example, if you have two years of experience as a Lotus Notes consultant, you may want to continue in Notes and build on the background you already have.

If you do choose to become involved in SAP, study the program and decide on what your particular SAP niche should be. SAP is a vast subject, allowing for many different areas of expertise. You should pursue the area of SAP that is most relevant to your current skills. If you are a programmer, consider getting training in ABAP/4, SAP's programming language. If you have an MBA and background in financial software, set your sights on becoming a functional consultant in the FI/CO modules. Choosing a logical area of focus will give your resume continuity when and if the SAP consulting market cools down.

In order to break into SAP consulting, you must address your professional inventory, how it will appear on a resume, and how you might leverage it into an SAP consulting destination. The elements in question are:

- Education level (for most positions, a university degree is a must)
- Previous professional experience
- Previous project experience
- Previous consulting experience
- SAP training
- SAP experience.

ELEMENT						
Degree	✔		✔		✔	✔
>3 yrs exp.	✔	✔				✔
Project experience	✔	✔				
SAP Training	✔	✔		✔	✔	
SAP Experience	✔	✔		✔		
DESTINATION						
Big Five	●	O	O	✣	O	O
Little 100	●	●	✣	O	O	✣
End-user	●	●	✣	O	O	O

● Good Shot   O Aim required   ✣ Long Shot

Now that you have chosen an area of SAP to focus on, you must find a way to get that experience. You need a strategy that will distinguish you from the hordes of others who are also approaching companies looking for SAP training and experience. As a general rule, the first mistake people make is to over-emphasize their desire for SAP training. Companies tend to view IS professionals who apply to their firm specifically for SAP training as opportunists, self-interested financial thrill-seekers who will move into any hot area in order to make a quick buck.

It is better to approach companies emphasizing the valuable skills you already have. One candidate we once spoke to had just botched his phone interview with a Big Five client. Later the candidate told us that instead of emphasizing his desire for SAP training he should have emphasized his extensive experience coordinating mainframe-to-client/server conversions. Exactly. Companies want to know that they are getting a return on their investment from the day you walk in the door.

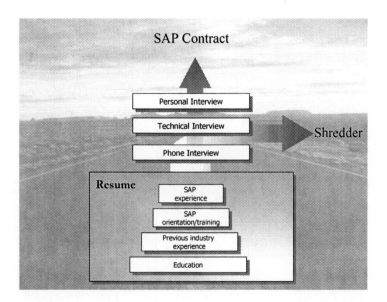

Your SAP employment strategy has to start from your current employment situation. If you are already with a company using SAP, you are in a much better position to secure SAP training or move into SAP consulting. The difficulty comes for those who are employed by companies that are not using SAP and have no plans to purchase the product. In this situation, you face two main choices: (1) pursue SAP training classes or (2) get yourself hired by a company that will give you "hands-on" exposure actually using the product.

C, C++, Java, Basic, and the Queen's English

A number of wannabe SAP consultants have asked us what language they should master before veering into an SAP career. This question belies their misguided notion that SAP is a technical, IS-based, arena. Our answer to the question is: you should master English.

One of the most common, and annoying, characteristics of new graduates who filter into industry is the contrast between their highly-developed technical skills and their inability to write a coherent paragraph. This is a drawback in any professional domain, but can be almost fatal in SAP consulting.

Technical skills alone are of little import. Consultants do not work in a vacuum and the ability to speak and to write in a clear manner (in brief, the ability *to express* what you know) will serve you in every aspect of your career.

Knocking on the SAP Door

Regardless of your level of SAP expertise, there comes a time when you need to take it upon yourself to market your services. If you have solid SAP experience, the easiest way to get your resume out is to select a recruiting firm and let specialists do what they do best: present your resume to key officials and get interviews lined up for you without delay. However, if you do not have SAP experience, you may find yourself short of professional assistance and without the industry contacts and reputation that help a more experienced SAP professional.

It takes time to market your services properly, but the experience of preparing your resume, doing some research and cold-calling is a valuable one for any job seeker to undertake. If you find yourself locked out of the opportunity to get SAP experience and not getting the opportunities you are looking for, you should take a broader view, and remember that the skills you are acquiring during this challenging search are essential for the modern job-seeker. Hard-won, yes, and not much fun to acquire in many cases, but essential nevertheless.

For technical professionals, the most important job tip to keep in mind is that if you can find a way to speak to the technical managers directly, you may have a much more effective route to your new position than those who go directly through human resources offices. Although many HR offices are very competent and responsible, HR personnel cannot be expected to understand your technical background and its potential significance to the company you are approaching. If you can find a graceful way of speaking directly to the technical manager who would be supervising you on the job, you have overcome a major hurdle in your job search.

At this point, the North American SAP market is shifting from a Fortune 500-Big Five axis to the middle and small markets. Business knowledge supersedes SAP background. Consulting skills are more in demand than before. In the mid 90s, SAP configuring skills alone qualified people for jobs in six figures. As we cross into the new millennium, broader and deeper skills will be needed if you are going to thrive.

Approaching SAP America

Due to continued rampant growth, SAP America is constantly looking for new employees at sales, consulting, and administrative levels. If you have a university degree, some years of industry background, and are willing to relocate, you might go directly to SAP America and hope they will give you a shot.

New SAP consultants need to have industry background in finance, logistics, manufacturing, or human resource or possess sufficient IS background (preferably in development and implementation). Those engaged by SAP are put through a rigorous ten week consulting academy which results in 'SAP consulting certification'.

Otherwise, you cannot receive training at SAP unless you are sponsored by a company with an official relationship with SAP America. Some ambitious self-starters have managed to take training courses by paying their own way through a company where they have personal contacts, even if they do not work there. This is a useful but expensive option which could run you ten thousand dollars or more. As a rule, training courses do not guarantee you employment. Indeed, many of those who have completed SAP training courses but do not have practical experience have a difficult time finding their first position.

Employment at SAP America usually means a re-location to:

- ❏ Philadelphia, PA
- ❏ Waltham, MA
- ❏ Atlanta, GA
- ❏ Foster City, CA
- ❏ Chicago, IL

Although SAP America has offices in other locales, these are the hubs.

Think long and hard before you quit a job to enroll in a month-long SAP course if the end in sight is employment at SAP. Your future employment there is by no means guaranteed. If, however, you can receive the course training without giving up your present position, or if you have the financial resources to obtain this training, it is a fairly sound investment.

It should also be noted that a career at SAP America can be very open-ended. Although no one can say with certainty how long the rampant growth of this company will continue, it is now possible to 'rise with the tide' as new opportunities and challenges appear on the SAP horizon. We have noted that few SAP employees remain in the same position for lengthy stretches as SAP America grows and transforms each year, from 200 employees in 1992 to more than 3,000 in 1998.

It is important to note that pay scales at SAP America are lower than SAP consultants will find in the consulting firms. However, employment at SAP America provides the opportunity to forge friendships and contacts that will be useful if ever you leave SAP.

Alternate Approaches

There is a practical approach to getting involved in SAP that seems to work better than the classic method of seeking training and then a position. This approach requires research and patience and gumption, but tends to yield better results. Further, following this tack allows you to maintain your current position until you have a firm offer.

First of all, realize that you are on your own, in that recruiting firms will probably not be very useful to you until you obtain SAP experience. In some cases, they may even be a hindrance. A company that is wavering on whether or not to hire you despite your lack of experience might end up passing on you if they have to pay a recruiting fee. Once you have some hands-on SAP experience, recruiting firms will be of more help to you in your job search.

But for now, you need to be prepared to contact companies on your own. You will have to take the extra time to market yourself and plan your approach. If you send out a generic resume with a cover letter indicating your desire to train in SAP, you are one of several thousand to do so and will probably not even get a call back. Even in today's 'here today, downsized tomorrow' environment, companies want team players, people who are genuinely interested in making a contribution to their firm. When you approach a company and emphasize your SAP goals, you tag yourself, like it or not, as self-interested, looking for a hot career area in order to make a financial killing.

A much better approach is to take stock of your skills, and research companies that use SAP in your industry or skill area. Develop a working list of companies that might be interested in the skills you already have. Research each company carefully, and learn all you can about their product, management philosophy, etc. Then, approach these firms based on your current skills and merits. For example, if you are a C++/GUI specialist, present yourself as such, and downplay your desire to get into SAP. Emphasize instead your interest in the company's mission, and what skills you can contribute (as in, how much money you can save them or what special skills you bring to the party?) the minute you walk in the door.

Once you have received a job offer from a company using SAP, you are in a much better situation. Go to work in your area of expertise, and set about proving your value and make a positive contribution. After a few months on the job, you will have proven your worth and made the internal contacts to have a much better shot at learning SAP. With any luck, your current duties will already dovetail with the SAP work that's being done.

Most of the people who now have solid SAP experience got their start by being in the right place at the right time. Example: one consultant we spoke to is contracting as an EDI specialist at a large SAP site. He is now working late nights on the SAP project, getting hands-on training from a manager who is more than happy to help him out, due to his excellent efforts in the EDI area. His only concern is his current consulting firm, which is asking for a higher rate for his services *because he now has SAP skills.*

This consultant was in the right place and made sure it was the right time by taking the initiative. It is a tactic that works. Using your current skills as leverage works because value is paramount, and SAP training expensive. Remind companies what you have to offer them now. Be patient. And keep up your good work in your designated area. When you do get a chance to gain SAP exposure, take what you can get, but remember not to get too involved in an area of SAP that is not directly tied to implementation, configuration, or technical experience. A hands-on background as a trainer or as a user is not nearly as valuable.

If for some reason you opt to pursue courses and certification and THEN look for hands-on experience, remember once again to select courses that will build on your current skills and background. And when you do get out of classes, find SAP-related work as soon as possible. Do not make the mistake of holding out for a higher rate because you were making more in Powerbuilder contracting before SAP. Take the first good position or contract you get. At this point the key is to get hands-on experience and to avoid time on the bench looking for the perfect position.

You will get better rates and salaries as you go, but avoid turning down offers unless you have other SAP options. One ABAP/4 certified programmer turned down a $40 per hour contract. He has yet to find another contract and has now resigned himself to returning to his previous position as a C++ programmer.

There is no one way to get involved in SAP. The key is to come up with a unique approach, one that separates you from the others who share your same goal. If you have a clear idea of how your SAP work will fit in with your long-term goals within the IS field, you will be much better off.

What SAP Training Will Do For You

Certainly any type of SAP training can be an asset to your career, but before investing your hard-earned cash, it is helpful to understand how that training is perceived by hiring officials in comparison to other aspects of your resume.

Before investing money in training, you should know that training in itself is no guarantee. Success for the entry-level SAP person depends less on the training itself and more on self-marketing and effective networking. To better understand the value of SAP training, you may want to review the following hierarchy of skills. Although there are no absolutes in the SAP world, these are the priorities for most hiring officials:

1. R/3 implementation experience. In the SAP market, hands-on R/3 implementation experience of some kind is still #1. Nothing is more valuable than having 'been there, done that.' The current minimum benchmark is a year of implementation experience focused in a specific technical or functional area. However, many of the more appealing SAP employment options, such as independent contracting or working for a smaller consulting firm, are closer to a two year minimum. We make a distinction here between implementation and user experience- the latter is not nearly as marketable.

2. R/2 implementation experience. Not generally as valuable as R/3 experience, but always worthwhile. Due to the difference between the mainframe and client-server setting, Basis skills may be a bit less transferable, but any R/2 experience is a help.

3. Consulting experience. Because so much of your success as an SAP consultant involves solid client-relations skills, previous consulting work, ideally in an SAP setting, is very helpful for most SAP positions. The prestige factor of the firm and the firm's clients is also a factor which carries weight.

4. Bachelor's degree. Although advanced degrees are not necessarily required for SAP positions, the lack of a bachelor's degree has prevented some top professionals from obtaining good positions. Even if the bachelor's degree is in an unrelated, non-technical area, it is still an asset, a sort of bottom line that can come into

play. Especially useful for those trying to process H-1 visa sponsorships.

5. Relevant industry or management experience. A decent number of SAP positions require at least two years of solid technical experience in related fields, such as an Oracle DBA background, or coding experience in other languages besides ABAP/4. SAP professionals who are only six months out of college can still find better positions than many of their former classmates, but there is no question that additional industry experience is an asset, both in terms of securing a position and in maximizing compensation.

6. Communications skills/personality. To IT folks, so-called 'communication skills' are often seen as a hazy area better off ignored. After all, are these not the kind of 'soft', undefined skills that always seem to show up as vague requirements on banal corporate job descriptions, right next to 'must be a team player?'

    In the brave new world of SAP, all of this changes. There are good reasons for polishing up your social skills. As the supply of experienced SAP consultants increases, communication skills are playing a more and more important role in the evaluation of SAP applicants. Instead of looking at communication skills as a 'soft' area that takes you away from your technical duties and into long, unnecessary meetings, think communication skills PLUS. The PLUS is the deep commitment to SAP as a vehicle for business change, and your commitment to seeing and achieving the client's 'big picture' goals. Communication skills PLUS means being able to think of your duties in terms of creating new, efficient business processes. This means being able to work with functional and technical team members, users, and higher level executives. You will not be able to hide in the cubicle anymore. Without this strong interpersonal foundation, there is a good chance you will not even get through the interview process.

The following areas could be considered the second tier- not essential for most positions, but certainly a plus:

7. Certifications from SAP America. Official certifications in ABAP/4 programming and other areas, while no guarantee of employment, can be an asset, particularly in conjunction with hands-on skills.

8. Experience as a user or SAP trainer. Although SAP user experience is not nearly as valuable as experience implementing and configuring the system, it can be an asset. If you continue to work as a user after your company's implementation is complete, it can add an additional component to your resume. But those applicants who came on only after the SAP system was up and running have a much more difficult time finding work than those who participated in the implementation itself. The same goes for trainers, unless the trainer also has SAP technical skills.

9. Additional relevant degrees. It is not essential to have a relevant degree to be a successful SAP consultant, but it definitely doesn't hurt, and in the case of senior level positions, having a Master's in Computer Science for technical positions, or an MBA for functional positions, can be a plus. It should be noted that the advanced degree can work against you if it means that your actual industry experience in information systems is light.

10. Non-SAP America training courses- the types of training courses the reader mentions above, sponsored not by SAP but by private companies, can be useful. But training stamped and certified by SAP is still the training with the most value.

Last and also least are SAP training courses in written and CD-ROM form. Neither is particularly valuable except as a learning tool. Fairly or not, self-education does not capture the attention of most SAP hiring officials.

The most useful training is clearly training that leads directly to experience that will allow training to be turned to practice.

You Are Your Resume

Voiceless, Faceless, Embraceable You

You would not show up for a job interview with your shoes untied, one button missing from your shirt, and your hair unbrushed. All the same, it is highly probable that you have unwittingly done just that when it comes to your resume.

If the destination is a consulting job or contract assignment, consider the following stages and where your face, voice, and perfectly knotted necktie appear:

1. Resume
2. Phone Interview
3. Personal Interview (Optional)
4. Negotiation
5. Agreement

In the majority of SAP contract assignments, step 3 never occurs. Time and distance do not allow for it. The first objective of your resume is to attract enough attention to get you to step 2. Once you do, your voice, personality, and experience come into play. Until that point, however, *you are your resume.* It is what they see first and sometimes it is all they will ever see. If they do not like what is on that resume, they will neither see you nor hear about your background and skills. You will be dead in the shredder.

Many SAP job searches are slowed down, hampered, or just plain killed by the submission of inappropriate resumes. If your recruiter or industry contact advises you to rewrite part of your resume for better impact, this is not an attempt to waste your time. Hiring officials are busy people. If they do not see what they are looking for on your resume, they may not bother to ask for details; details you might have been able to provide, if only you had known.

Staffing happens fast in the world of SAP. Actually, there are three stages: hurry up, wait, hurry up. You do not always have the luxury of a personal interview (face-to-face) and the decision to offer you a phone interview is almost entirely based upon *the look and content of your resume.*

Here are some tips and reminders for those of you who are working on or updating your resumes. These are not provided as an insult to anyone's intelligence, just as a reminder that nobody's perfect, and a first impression can be hard to reverse.

Resume Structure

All great stories and all great movies have a common element: the solid structure of a beginning, a middle, and an end. Your resume is your story, your version of events. Tell it well.

The maximum length of your standard resume is two pages. The minimum length of your standard resume is two pages. If your experience and education cannot at least fill a page and have a spillover of at least a third of a second page, you might appear, well, light as air.

On the other hand, it may be difficult to cram the totality of your background into two pages. Still, do it. What you must do is cut to the chase of who you are, what you have done, and where and when you did it. If you succeed at this, you will almost certainly reach your goal, which is a phone interview, during which the salient details of your experience can be related.

Some people will want more and you should always include the phrase "Further details on request." To satisfy such a request, create a second, fully detailed resume (e.g. up to four or five pages). What you want to avoid is the overkill of too much detail. Even if you have extensive SAP experience, the content on two pages will suffice to project it. Indeed, simply by putting on the heading 'SAP Experience: 3 Years' you will get the attention you are seeking.

Heading: Name, Coordinates	15 %
SAP Background	50%
Other Professional Background	25%
Training & Education:	10%

Repeat your name and phone/fax data on the second page for when the two pages get separated (they will, trust us).

Heading 15%   - the title and cast of the story

SAP Body 50% Plotline A: what we care about

Other Professional 25% Plotline B: character depth

Training/Education 10% Career path map.

Showcase Your SAP Background

The most important rule: if you are seeking an SAP-related position, your SAP experience should be emphasized in significant detail near the top of your resume.

Ideally, this will take the form of a detailed breakdown of your current job in SAP. It is often helpful, in addition to a specific review of your various duties, to include a bold-typed list of the modules and technical expertise used in each assignment. If your SAP experience spans many jobs and assignments, you may want to begin your resume with a summary of your skills and/or include a one-page summary of your significant SAP-related achievements.

If your current position is not in SAP, you need to de-emphasize your current position and detail/highlight the position in which you did use SAP. If you have only received SAP training, then you may want to bring this training information towards the front of the resume and break down what you've been trained/certified to do. However, if you have SAP industry experience as well as training, your training should go at the end of your resume.

Other Professional Background

Do not waste a lot of paper detailing your non-SAP duties in this resume, unless they have direct relevance to the type of SAP position you are looking for. Example: you may want to detail some of your relevant consulting skills or programming background, but remember that you need to showcase your SAP skills in this resume; all else is distraction. The most common reason a recruiter or consulting firm returns a resume to an applicant to be rewritten is the need for more SAP detail and a more prominent location for SAP-related skills on the resume.

If you can quantify your skills in dollars and cents and/or in terms of project completion, do so. If you know how much your implementation saved your client in terms of a percentage of operating expenses or dollars saved, include this type of information. If you managed a project to completion, be as specific as possible about the timeline you were given and the date you finished. Companies like to know that you understand the financial bottom line that your skills will bring their organization. If you aided in the development of your company's client base, be specific about the revenues gained or the size and number of clients added. Remember though, that numbers do not lie. Be only as specific as can be verified.

Include all Bachelor's and Master's degrees somewhere on the resume, preferably at the end. Include your grade point/academic honors only if they are exceptional. Be careful about including an objective; too often this statement limits your scope and distracts from the key SAP information that should appear near the top.

Do not include personal information such as hobbies. One applicant recently sent in a resume that included, under interests, paint gun expert. This type of personal information almost never works in your favor on paper.

Customizing Your Resume

If at all possible, customize your resume to match the needs of each company or industry type you are pursuing each time you send it out. If you know previous consulting experience is important, emphasize that. If you know that the company is considering the PP module, point out your PP experience clearly.

Presentation

Don't make your type too small. A ten-point font is the smallest you should go, twelve points is often better. Try to resist the temptation to show off your font collection. Pick one or two nice, easy to read fonts, one for headings and another for base text. AVOID THE USE OF CAPS, EXCEPT FOR HEADINGS.

Do *not* over-use *emphatic italics* or **bold within text** to underscore *important* features, nor should any exclamation marks be necessary!! Italics, embedded bold, and exclamation marks add shrillness, not import.

About Your Electronic Image

No matter how wonderful your photo may be, no matter what professional gloss it may project, you will appear to be a member of a Georgia chain gang once that photo has been faxed, photocopied, and faxed again.

Black is My Favorite Color

With the explosion of color in recent years, it is now a breeze to create elegant colorized resumes. This is fine if you are in a position to mail your resume around or, better, take it along with you to prospective clients.

In the majority of cases, there will not be time enough for regular mail and not everyone will be in a position to download your Word e-mail attachment and print it cleanly on their HP Deskjet. Instead, your resume will follow a treacherous route:

- It will be faxed
- The fax will be photocopied
- Coffee will be spilled onto the original
- The photocopy will be faxed
- The receiving fax will jam momentarily and your second page will come out slanted.

Even graceful use of gray tones is almost useless because of the transmission/copy splash effect. The color blue resists faxing and photocopying. Its effect is a very light, nearly illegible gray.

In the same harsh light, do not use gray paper or any paper with background. What you want is black print on a clean white field so that fax and photocopy distortions will be kept to a minimum.

Check Your Work

Always proofread before you send out. Too many resumes are sent out with typos. A typographical error has the same effect on your target as would an un-buttoned shert. (Get the point?)

Can I Get a Witness From the Congregation?

With so much $ in SAP, there are a lot of bogus resumes floating around and recruiters can all recount stories of how they have been burned. References count more for SAP candidates than in most other sectors of business.

If you are already an SAP consultant, be sure to obtain a written reference at every stop in your project work. You should also obtain permission from your client contact to use them for phone references. These *will* be checked.

If you are trying to break into SAP, gather references from previous jobs or projects that will put you in a good light. The ability to work in teams and with clients is almost as important as the technical or business content of your background, so references that are favorable to your 'consulting/teamwork' skills will give you an edge.

Web Site Resumes

We know a number of consultants who maintain web sites and post their resumes on them. This is an excellent idea but one that can yield negative results if the idea is misused. For example, one consultant steadfastly refuses to fax a resume, citing that it is right there on the net, just go get it and download it. Some of us are modern, some of us are troglodytes with scarcely used keyboards. And troglodytes do a lot of SAP hiring. If you insist that you can only be found on the Net, you will be lost.

In another instance, an SAP consultant's web site is a mix of personal and professional. He includes photos of his apartment complex, his car, himself with friends, etc. and offers more than you want to know about his personal interests. "Charlie Parker is my idol!" Uh huh. Click to exit.

The best site we have found was put up by a Basis consultant in the Bay Area. The site offers a front page summary of skills and career direction and there are three ways to access the resume: online, in Word format, or in text format. Simple, attractive, and to the point. This man was recruited to the job he wanted in the city he preferred for the salary he was seeking in the space of days.

Other Media - Oh, Please, No

You want to distinguish yourself, you want your candidacy to be memorable and attractive, but you wonder if the content of your resume is lacking. You consider various gambits, little extras that will fix you in the mind of a recruiter. Like these?

Video tapes=you want to be in soaps?
Audio tapes=you want to be a DJ?

CD Rom=over the top.
PowerPoint Presentation=nope.
Six-color resume: the peacock fantail.

When recruiters receive such exotica, the effect is just the opposite of what you are hoping. This extra 'plumage' seems silly and desperate. The bottom line: if the black and white of the resume do not suffice, no artifice will bridge the gap.

In conclusion, a resume that follows these guidelines will not only pave the way to better interviews, it will undoubtedly make money for you.

Sample SAP resume - target: full-time employment

Jennifer Sapphire Sofun
101 Midway
New York, NY 10024
Phone (212) 999-9999 Fax (212) 999-9998 E-mail sofun@cool.com

SAP Expertise: FI/CO Module Leader
SAP Experience: 3 Years
Industry Experience: 5 Years
SAP Background

Ace Place   New York   April, 1997 to present
Position: FI/CO module lead

Responsible for implementation FI/CO team at client implementing R/3 v. 3.1 for global rollout of FI, CO, SD, MM, and HR.

Beta Shop   Chicago   June, 1996 - March, 1997
Position: FI configuring

As part of a 6 member team under the direction of a Big 5 project manager, I assisted in the configuration of the FI module for a billion dollar squeegee manufacturing firm. This implementation resulted in an immediate savings of more than $60M due to reduced lead times and

Gamma Consulting   Chicago   Aug, 1992 - May, 1996
Final position: Sr. SAP Consultant

In nearly four years I progressed from a C+ programmer to ABAP/4 (financial applications) to FI consultant. I took part in three R/3 implementations, all at Fortune 500 sites, and all on time and on budget.

- Gigacorp (Chicago) FI configuration
- Bulge Inc. (LaSalle, Ill.) FI instruction to 60 end-users
- Fat City (Decatur, Ill.) FI/CO configuration - EDI design

Education   Lilliput University BA in Computer Sciences, 1991.

Getting into the Right SAP Game

Unless you are a first-timer, the question is not just getting into the SAP game, but getting into the right SAP game. As gratifying as it may be to receive multiple offers, the only offers that matter are those that would place you in a position to succeed.

Assuming your resume is up to snuff and you have skills and background that are sought, you will find yourself in the unsurprising position of being asked to talk it over. Amazingly, there are vast numbers of experienced, solid SAP consultants who cannot grasp the fact that it is not enough to toss a resume into the ring. Their frustration levels rise the second they are asked questions based on the resume. "I did that," one candidate once answered us. "It says so right there on page two."

Score one for SAP background. Take back two for lack of social skills. This guy met the shredder.

There are two types of interviews and each requires different preparation and mind-set:

- The phone interview
- The personal interview.

Phone Interviews

The purpose of the SAP phone interview varies according to the type of position you are applying for. If you are being considered for a permanent position, you may go through several phone interviews, hoops you must get through if you hope to obtain an in-person interview. If you are interviewing for a contract assignment, the phone interview may be the only interview you receive. If a consulting firm is considering you for a contract assignment, you may be interviewed by a hiring manager, the president of the consulting firm, and may even meet with the client...all over the phone.

The Interview Chain

	Permanent	Contract
1 Screen Interview	Recruiter	Placement Spec
2 General Interview	General Manager	Project Manager
3 Technical Interview	Module specialist	Module specialist
4 Formal Interview	General Manager	Seldom occurs
5,6,7.... (Confirming Interviews)	Partners, colleagues	Seldom occurs
Reference Checks	Variable	Too seldom occurs

You may be working through a recruiter, or applying for positions directly, but the same general principles apply in either situation. Your recruiter can be helpful to you by letting you know their client will be calling you, and giving you a feel for the company and their hiring process. Either way, your first goal is to understand this company's approach: how many phone interviews take place, which ones will be technical in nature, and who will be calling?

Surprises are best avoided. Sometimes you will answer a ringing telephone and, with no warning, find yourself talking to a potential client. You are in the middle of a project, and suddenly you are on the spot. Depending on the confidentiality of your work setting, you may not even be able to talk at work. Unless you are confident you will not be interrupted and you have a good idea of the type of position you are being interviewed for, it is usually better to set up another time to talk. Once your phone interview is set up, you can call your recruiter and otherwise prepare for the next hurdle in the hiring process: the phone screen.

The General Screen

If you are applying for a permanent position, and you know that your goal is an in-person interview further down the line, it is good to keep in mind the golden rule: *do not talk money over the phone*. During this first phone call, you will probably be interviewed by a general hiring manager. Technical questions will not be too rigorous just yet. The goal at this point is for the company to get a general idea of your skills and goals. During the first interview, it is useful to be prepared for technical questions, but the key to the first phone interview is to have an engaging, comfortable discussion with the hiring official. The most important thing during this exploratory conversation is to stay loose and relaxed. Remember not to ramble during your responses, and save your questions until the latter part of this interview.

Quite often, client myopia is the toughest of your obstacles. Because of the depth and width of SAP R/3, there is a lot of specialization and too many clients tend to focus on experience in a single module (or sub-module) to the exclusion of all else.

Here is the paraphrase of a conversation we had in early 1997:

> Client: I need someone with at least one year of experience in SAP HR.
>
> Us: I'm sorry. The HR module of R/3 was only released six months ago. We have someone with five months of experience.
>
> Client: I need someone with a *full year*.
>
> Us: No one has a full year of HR experience. As we said, the HR module of R/3 was only released *six months ago*.

Client: I gotta have at least *one full year* of HR experience.

Us: No one on this planet has a full year of HR experience.

Client: I'll just keep asking around.

You may find it necessary to educate the client during the course of your interview. Often, the person interviewing you at this point knows little or nothing about SAP and is merely "filling a slot" on the request of someone else. If you are able to re-frame off-the-mark questions in a polite way, you may score more points than otherwise.

One great advantage of the phone interview is that you do not have to worry about the visual aspects of your appearance. As long as you don't talk too fast, you can stay focused on the essence of the conversation. This is especially useful during the next phase of the typical phone interview, the technical screen.

The Technical Screen

During your technical interview, you should have at your fingertips detailed information about your technical skills and accomplishments. These could include project outlines, performance reviews, and a general summary of your technical skills that you yourself have put together. No one can tell if you are glancing at your paperwork, at least not at this point in the digital revolution. It can give you a real sense of security to know that if you get the jitters during your technical interview, help is just one glance away.

Passing the technical screen means fulfilling the expectations of your client, not showing off what you know. This is why it is so critical to know what the client wants. We know a senior Basis consultant who has light exposure to Correction and Transport from a year previous, but for the most part has supervised others who were working in this area. A potential client had a strong need for Correction and Transport skills. If our man had known what the client really needed, he could have brushed up on these skills, hit the books, and come off sounding knowledgeable. This did not occur and the client opted for a junior-level person who happened to have more recent experience in this area. Both consultant and client, in this case, lost out.

Typically, once the technical screen has been passed, the company will want to bring you in for an in-person meeting. However, things are a bit different if you are doing the entire process over the phone.

If the decision to hire is based solely on phone conversations, the next phase is going to be rate or salary negotiation. Remember that if you can meet in-person with your client before you talk money, it will usually work out better. In either case, remember what we have advised before: keep the focus on impressing the client. Once your client is chafing at the bit to hire you, and ideally has made you an offer, then you can talk about per diems, flying home on weekends, or whatever else you feel is necessary in order to accept the position.

But even if you call the shots in the SAP market, you should do everything you can to avoid coming off like a mercenary. You might want to give out your last rate or salary and suggest that you are open to a fair increase from your most recent salary. Do NOT say things like 'whatever the market will bear' even if that is your innermost attitude.

The following principles of SAP phone interviews warrant your review:

Set the right image. Because you are not meeting in person, the interviewer can only judge you based on your voice. Don't have anything in your mouth, don't smoke, and remember that background noise can carry quite well over the phone. (If you are at home and your dog starts barking, just tell the interviewer it is your client. Something to defuse the situation.)

The only appropriate thing to do while you are on a phone interview is to review your notes at your desk. Do not try to catch up on the dishes. It's been tried before, and is never effective. Save experiments in multi-tasking for phone conversations with relatives. Speak clearly, and slightly more slowly than usual. Remember that without visual cues, the only enthusiasm a client can pick up is your voice.

Prepare well. Use the phone interview to your advantage. Have facts like your work history and technical skills in front of you, so you do not find yourself scrolling around through your memory. If you have questions for the client, have those written down as well.

Avoid salary talk. Postpone all talk of money, benefits, vacation, or anything that would seem selfish and self-interested UNTIL you have some type of offer letter in hand. A recruiter can be very useful getting this information handled and relayed to the client, but if you are on your own, wait and negotiate when an offer has been made. Your SAP skills put you in the driver's seat, but during your interviews emphasize what you have to offer, not what you want to gain.

Maintain a positive tone, particularly when you are asked your reasons for leaving a current or previous job. Keep the focus in terms of where you want to go with your career, not what you dislike about where you are. Remember that while your reason for leaving should be positive, it should also be persuasive. Companies want to know you are ready to move on.

We very recently came upon a candidate with a sterling silver resume, a solid combo of business background, consulting bones, and SAP steel. Further, he had years upon years of international experience and our client was in need of just this profile.

Unfortunately, he peppered his phone interview with phrases like, "I've been trying to get us moving in an international direction, but these cretins I'm working with don't get it."

Der schredder, la shreddair, el shreddo, it's all the same to us.

Request a personal interview. Sometimes, nothing is more effective than simply letting a company know you are interested in them and ready to go. At the end of the conversation, you may want to ask for an in-person meeting, an opportunity to meet face-to-face. In the heat of the moment, if you have set a good tone, your interviewer may simply say yes, sparing you from a cold evaluation session later in the day as the interviewer tries to remember why he/she liked you while the boss scrutinizes your resume.

The Personal Interview

Preparing for the Interview

In the days preceding an interview, tie up all loose logistical ends. Call and reconfirm interview times. Make sure you have an up-to- date schedule of all the people you will see. Seek to remember job titles and responsibilities. If the woman who is to interview you has a name like Akhnakatovna Bjeserminq, strive to pronounce it correctly. Nothing is more awkward than finding yourself in a surprise meeting with the president of the company when you were not prepared for her/him. Verify flight arrangements if necessary, plan your travel time up until the point you will walk in the company's door, making sure that there will be no tight points where a slight delay in your flight or drive could set your interview off with a late arrival.

Once the logistics are set, gather and review the information you have obtained on the company. Hopefully by now, through your phone interviews, you have gained some knowledge about this company's particular SAP project and what your role there might be. If you do not have enough background, get onto the Internet and dig for more. Keep notes. Remember that the HR people in most firms have to repeat the base info about their companies on a regular basis.

"Our firm was founded in 1712 by pygmy Puritans from the Isle of Wight. Today we employ 14,400 people in 16 countries and have been listed on NASDAQ since the year Aunt Cheechee took over as CEO."

It is refreshing for HR people when prospective candidates already know all this.

Italicized advice: the more you know about your prospective employer, the better impression you will make.

You will almost always need to bring a list of references, usually three. It is better to mix these references, such as one supervisor, one co-worker, and one personal reference. Reference expectations vary from company to company, so check on this ahead of time. Find out if the company expects you to fill out the application ahead of time, and verify all of the materials that they want you to bring. The company may also request verification of income. If they do, make sure you also indicate any bonuses or hidden benefits that affect your salary. Make sure you take the time to pick up or dry clean the right clothes. Picking up those little interview aids like breath mints doesn't hurt either. Have a few fresh copies of your resume ready to bring to the interview that day.

On the day/night before your interview, it is best to set aside an hour or more to make a written plan for the next day. There is no substitute for this quiet time with pen/laptop computer in hand. It is best to do this late afternoon, early evening, in case you have any last minute questions as a result of this final preparation. Have an evening number handy, in case you have any questions the night before or some emergency has come up.

Make a list of the various experiences and capabilities you have which will be an asset to them if you are hired. Review your possible responses to difficult interview questions. Some of the more difficult questions include:

- What are your strengths and weaknesses?
- Why do you want to leave your current position?

- How do your spouse and children feel about this career move? (especially important if this job involves relocation or extensive travel)
- What do you know about our company?
- What are your short term and long term goals?

Obviously, you have given a lot of thought to each of these questions and so you feel prepared to discuss them in an interview. Thought is not sufficient preparation. Interview yourself aloud, and answer these questions, aloud. How do you sound? Was it a six-uhs-per-sentence response? If so, work it out until you have reduced it to a one or fewer uh-per-sentence answer.

Now that you are ready to focus, clarify your main objective, which is to obtain an offer from this company by making as good an impression as possible. Whether or not you end up wanting to work with this firm, you still want to obtain a promising offer. Perhaps the other job you have lined up will fall through, or this company may come up with a compensation package you cannot refuse. So keep your goal in focus: go for that offer. Write up or review what you know about their particular SAP needs.

The Day of the Interview

The in-person interview invokes your basic abilities to communicate and present yourself. At this point, you have probably had a technical phone interview and the company is prepared to hire you, assuming all goes well. Since you have already prepared and probably have a handle on dressing yourself properly, we'll go through these in-person tips quickly, just hitting the most important ones, in chronological order:

- Take your time in the morning, so that you don't forget all of the things you will need that day, such as references, resumes, directions to the company site, etc.

- Leave for the interview EARLY. Allow plenty of time for any delays. (One of the authors, unspecified here, always gets lost at least once on the way to a new office. He learned long ago to leave *really early* for important interviews.)

- If time permits, get to a restroom when you arrive. Check your face and clothing to be sure that you have not had your appearance altered in commute and that you do not have that deer caught in the headlights glaze in your eyes.

You are prepared. Groomed, schooled, rehearsed, breath-minted, and hyped. If you are kept waiting beyond the scheduled interview time, have something to read with you. There is nothing more annoying to a receptionist than some poor soul sitting there in a pool of sweat, biting the last fingernail because Mr. Coolidge is making him wait. Keeping a candidate on ice is even a tactic of some firms, while the receptionist is making notes on the candidate's agitated behavior.

We were just kidding about that last part. The receptionists seldom take notes.

In the Cockpit: The Personal/Professional Interview

The Tip-Off

The time has come and your interrogator arrives. It is time for the handshake and need we remind you not to use either your commando death grip or your dishrag flop? OK, we will not even mention the importance of eye contact. Hey, even Pauly Shore understands the importance of eye contact.

And now is the time to have mastered the respiratory-vocal combination. People have a tendency to talk too fast during interviews. Take your time, speak clearly, do not forget to breathe.

Sit where you are told to sit. Do not play the geometry game and insist on standing. If coffee is offered and you want coffee, say so, and add (before being asked) how you take it. Do not insist on a caffe latte or a mocha unless you are interviewing with Starbucks. Black, with cream or sugar, or both.

After the small talk and the serving of coffee in a styrofoam cup, the main event begins. Either the interviewer will begin with a tour of the firm in question or with questions about you and your background. Take it in whichever order it comes. If the subject is the firm, concentrate on that subject first. Your time to shine will come.

Most of the difficult questions, such as "What do you know about our company," or "Why should we hire you," are easily addressed with proper preparation. If you get the five year plan question, always be a bit vague. NEVER say you want to be a manager. You may inspire some job insecurity in the manager who is interviewing you. Typically, the hardest questions to answer are those that invite a negative answer, such as strength and weaknesses, or "How do you like working with your current supervisor?"

The general rule is to turn these questions into positives without completely glossing them over. For example, one safe weakness would be your tendency to get wrapped up in a project and work too hard, not leaving time for family and rest. To an employer, this could very well be seen in a positive light, and yet it still shows an honest self-awareness. Obviously, you may face questions about salary, so prepare yourself for this but do not leap into discussions of pay.

The best time to talk about money is AFTER the company wants you. Make them want you before getting into such subjects.

Since a premature discussion of salary puts the chances of your getting an offer in jeopardy, and since your goal is to get an offer out of this company, you want to redirect these questions. Even if your primary concern is money, if this is raised during the interview do your best to reframe the discussion by making it clear that your primary goal is a good professional opportunity. Be prepared to say that a fair increase will be fine with you, but that you make your job decisions based on an overall view of the company and the opportunity, and not salary. This is music to a hiring official's ears. Once again, the BEST time to handle a salary negotiation is after the company has made it clear that they want you, and you are confident that they know what your skills will be worth to them.

Your focus during the bulk of the interview will be to keep emphasizing and expanding on what your business, consulting, and SAP skills could bring to this company. Personalize your approach to match this company's needs, and be as specific as possible about the delivery times of your previous implementations, problems and glitches you have resolved, etc.

At some point in the interview, beginning or middle or end, be sure to ask key questions about the firm. At base is, why would you want to work there? What does the firm have to offer you? If you are interviewing for an implementation position as part of an implementing firm and have concerns about this company's long-term commitment to SAP, *ask*. If you a consulting firm is courting you, it would be wise to ask about current engagements, target markets, marketing efforts, and the like. If you are talking to someone in a smaller consulting firm, be sure to ask whether or not you would be expected to accept consulting assignments (as opposed to being part of that firm's implementing team).

Let's face it. In nine out of ten such interviews, both parties are doing their best to show a friendly and positive face. Both of you want to like each other, to find a common fit. Otherwise, the interview is simply lost time. Do not fall into the slumber that such an atmosphere can induce. You are being investigated and you should also be investigating the firm in question.

The best way to impress is by researching each company you interview with. Try to get a feel for their particular SAP needs and make it clear just how you will be able to fill them. Keep in mind that your SAP job involves both technical and communication skills, and both will be evaluated during your interview. Especially if you are interviewing to be a consultant, your communication skills and ability to solve the human workflow problems that SAP implementations create are important.

For those of you who are H-1's looking for U.S. positions, remember to communicate clearly and with the best English you've got. As previously stated, people talk too fast during interviews. Most SAP positions involve client relations; your abilities to communicate clearly are vital to your chances.

It would be over the top to have a laundry list of questions just for the interview, but in asking such questions, you fulfill two purposes with one tactic:

- You learn about the company that is seeking to hire you
- You demonstrate that you are not to be had for money alone.

The opportunity to ask questions is too often overlooked. The best questions to ask are ones that implicitly show your knowledge of SAP and this company's particular challenges, such as: "Who is responsible for training and supervising the ABAP programming team," etc.

Once you have exhausted your questions and the interviewer is finishing interrogating you, the crossroads appear. Often, the interviewer will propose a break, during which thought is given to the offer that might be tendered. With or without a time break, you have to know what is coming next.

How to Talk Money and Get What You Want

The best time to talk about money is AFTER the company wants you. And they can't "fall" for you if you screen yourself out with a "what's in it for me?" premature discussion of salary.

The second biggest mistake SAP professionals make during interview sessions is resting on their professional laurels. While it is true that the SAP hiring market is largely controlled by the job-seekers, not the companies, most companies are wary of stories/tall tales they have heard about hit-and-run SAP contractors and want to know that you are genuinely interested in working for them.

The biggest mistake is cutting to the mercenary chase and talking dollars and cents prematurely.

Once you are ready to launch this part of the deal, be sure to have a checklist of negotiating points on hand. You may not get the base salary you were hoping for, but through careful negotiation you might well come ahead. Base salary is only a part of what you should be seeking. Do not choose one job over another because of a measly $10,000 difference in base salary. Over a three, four, or five-year stretch, the benefits packages, vacations, and training alone can dwarf the difference in base pay.

Negotiating Points (beyond base salary)

Benefits
> Health/Dental
> Life Insurance
> Retirement/Investment Plan

Bonuses
> Travel
> Performance
> Fixed

Travel and Expenses
> As Incurred
> Per Diem

Vacation

Relocation (if and when)

Training Provided (Guaranteed or Promised)

Material Provided (laptop, software, etc.)

Career Path

Trial Period

Job Assignments (what leverage do you have to accept or reject a proposed assignment?)

The SAP hiring market creates some unique and sensitive tension during the interview process. In some cases, the SAP applicant is going to enter at a higher salary level than the people who are interviewing him/her, a very tricky dynamic. You should be aware of the possibility that the hiring officials you are dealing with (especially if you are going through a human resources department) have probably worked years to achieve a benefits package/salary inferior to the type you already enjoy and want to equal or improve.

The key here is not to settle for less, but to be sensitive to the needs and concerns of the company until they are sold on your services. The best time to negotiate fine points in the benefits package, salary, or the 401K plan is AFTER you have had a good in-person interview, or at the very least after your technical skills and value to the company are both firmly established.

It is also important to not make a big show during the interview of all the other companies with which you have interviewed and the many offers you have received. Such an attitude leads quite naturally to a suspicion about you, as in, "Well, Mr. Satin, you have an impressive track record with successful projects in Buenos Aires, Monaco, and Puerto Vallarta. You also have huge offers from IBM, Price Waterhouse, and the Royal Saudi Family. Tell me, Mr. Satin, why would you give all that up to join little old us here in Milwaukee?"

As an SAP professional, you may be worth a lot, you may even be in control. Once this is established, there is no need to dig it in.

The classic rule is that the first person to name the price loses. In practice, this can be tricky. The company may be very determined to obtain your salary expectations before naming a figure.

SAP hiring officials may raise the question of salary early on, perhaps even in your first phone interview, to make sure that they can afford the serious resume they see in front of them. If you are an SAP candidate, you may welcome this discussion of money - at least you will know for certain whether or not this company can meet your salary expectations - before you take a day off from work for the interview.

There are many ways of tactfully handling the question of money if it is raised. Usually, it is best to come up with your own comments that echo the following sentiment: "At this point in my job search, I'm looking for the opportunity to expand/build-on my SAP skills in the [insert your expertise] area. Although I would like to receive a fair offer just like everyone else, my main goal is to find the right professional fit. So far, your company has a lot to offer in the [insert your expertise] area. I'm sure that we'll be able to settle on a pay scale that's fair for both of us, but right now I'd like to tell you about the skills I can bring to your organization."

If your interviewer presses you on the specifics of the money you are looking for, and clearly wants you to name a price, one possible approach is to mention the rate or salary you are making now, and say that you want a fair increase from that. Never mention the offer amounts you've been given by other firms. There are many reasons for this:

a)   This interview is not about other situations, and no two situations can ever be reduced strictly to financial factors.

b)   The question of retention of new consultants is more and more in the forefront; too many SAP consultants have job-hopped in past years. If you try to leverage for more money, you are shouting out that money is your primary element of decision and the pursuit may end right there. No one wants to hire you with the notion that you could have had a pile more money elsewhere.

c)   Unless you are merely in a mercenary posture, you should be looking to create the foundation for a major part of your career. If you inevitably stay with the firm for only two or three years, you will be better served if you have carved out a situation in which you can succeed and grow than if you merely grab the brass ring.

d)   Money in SAP is a given. Unless the initial offer is truly short of your expectations, you may express this. It could be that the employer has the wrong idea of your worth. It may be that you have the wrong idea of your true worth. You may have to simply sever the negotiations.

If you are transitioning to low travel, you may even want to emphasize your willingness to look at less pay for the quality of life a low-travel position can provide. Even a contractor, who is understood to be looking for an hourly rate, can benefit from this approach. Like many other contractors, you might have chosen that route primarily for the money, but in your interviews, focus on the skills you have to offer and the challenges you can meet for your new company. If you can honestly say that salary is not the only key issue, you will be sending a welcome signal to the client.

During your interview, simple things like stressing your enthusiasm for the firm will set the right tone, and create the best atmosphere for a later talk about salary. Ideally, this talk will take place after, or at least at the very end, of your in-person interview. Once a company wants you, you can be the negotiator you have wanted to be all along. In some cases, you might even turn down an offer that was less than you expected, only to see the company turn around a few days later and offer you $10,000 more than they said they were willing to pay. As a rare, special SAP professional, you may well be calling the shots in this job market, but you would do better to conduct yourself as if the opposite is the case.

Although the technical standards applied to SAP hires are becoming stricter (it is more difficult to obtain an SAP position unless you have at least six months of experience) the vast majority of unsuccessful applications are due not to lack of technical skill but to slip-ups during the interview process.

Closure

Many of the following tips will seem very basic, but are not meant to be condescending. Most of the tactics that will give you an edge over other applicants during your face-to-face interview are surprisingly simple.

At the end of the interview, ask for the job. This is very important. Shake the hiring official's hand, and state clearly your interest in the company and the position. This may feel a bit gung-ho for you, but it will make a major and lasting impression. Even if you have some misgivings about the firm, give some indication of your continuing interest.

Pick up business cards as you go if you do not already have them, so that you have addresses and names and job titles of the key people who interviewed you.

Within 48 hours or less, write a thank you note. Thank them for the opportunity, and once again re-emphasize your interest in the company. Remember this: less than an hour after your interview, you are already history. Business just keeps coming, as much for the interviewer as for you. By sending along this note, you are igniting the interviewer's memory of you in a positive way. This is not a Hallmark card, this is the trigger to a solid offer. Include something specific and memorable in your note. It is your coda, your asterisk, your last tossed flower.

Go home, relax, and debrief. If you are using an agency, this is a good time to call and report the highlights of the interview. Your agency can help you work out the fine points of the offer from a more neutral vantage point. In addition, they can be instrumental in ironing out any misunderstandings that occurred during the interview, and will probably know before you do how your interviewer felt about the event.

You may have another interview in a day or two. If so, go back to the beginning of this chapter and start again.

Handing off the Flame: SAP Education

Of Premium Value and Unfair Rewards

The Catch-22 of SAP: there are not enough trained consultants because those who have training are consulting and none of them are teaching.

The massive shortfall of experienced SAP consultants has grabbed the headlines over the past five years, but an even worse shortfall exists in the realm of SAP education and training.

Economics are at the core of this problem, and are simply explained. An SAP consultant can earn more than $150 per hour when assigned to implementation. That same consultant, if converted to a training specialist, will make significantly less. Implementations are adrenalin-driven affairs with deadlines and risk. SAP training is viewed as less time-impeded, and is incredibly undervalued. If you do not insist upon making a six figure salary and wish to have some control over the level of travel that you must endure, AND you have teaching skills and a sense of generosity, you can have a sweet career in this very necessary field of SAP.

Patti Walsh, who has ten years of SAP experience as a user, consultant, and instructor, makes the following point: "In today's market, consulting is more measurable than training, billable hours and all that. Teaching is harder to measure. Classroom time is minimal compared to the preparation time leading to the classroom. And more to the point, how do you measure a knowledge transfer?"

SAP America's training courses are notoriously uneven in quality and the quiet little secret is that SAP itself is seriously understaffed and subcontracts for a large portion of its off-site course delivery. Often, the courses are taught by people who have no implementation experience but have gone through a trainer- trains-the-trainer-program. With all respect, this is a 'hearsay' based, woefully academic, and clearly insufficient means of delivery. In other instances, experienced consultants who have no teaching skills are used. This is an even less satisfactory state of affairs.

It is evident that in the near term (1999-2000) the problem will merely continue. The shortfall might even carry well into the next millennium if implementation consulting continues to predominate. We often read articles about how clients are stressing internal SAP education as a means of reducing consulting costs, but we see too little evidence of this in the field.

Various SAP Training Levels

Here is a one of the queries we have received:

> "I am an SAP trainer. I have strong experience training my company's users in SD and MM, but I do not have implementation skills. You have some training jobs, but more implementation jobs. How do my skills fit in?"

This person is in the field of end-user training, which is only one of varying levels in the SAP education bookshelf:

Management education is the orphan of the SAP world. Although SAP markets directly to CEOs and CFOs and these are the people who tend to greenlight an SAP implementation, they seldom care to take the time to educate themselves, assuming that whatever they have learned in the pre-sales phase is sufficient. Many come back for education if their implementations go awry, but it is impossible to plan a career while waiting for these people to wise up, so cross this off your list as a viable consulting option.

Level	Typical Duration
Management Education	1 to 2 days
SAP Module	6 to 10 weeks
ABAP	4 to 6 weeks
End-user	1 to 2 weeks

Teaching courses for the various SAP modules can be lucrative and relatively rewarding if you hook up with SAP America as a subcontractor. To do so, while avoiding excessive travel, you should live close to Philadelphia, Chicago, Atlanta, Dallas, or Foster City, CA.

Other avenues for module instruction are within the Big Five, most notably PriceWaterhouseCoopers, ICS-Deloitte, and Ernst & Young, all of which have created SAP competency centers. In the next tier of consulting firms, the opportunities for work in SAP education are fairly shaky. If you surf the Net for SAP consulting firms, you will find that every single one of them list SAP training among their services. Once you scratch the surface, however, you find that, well, they've given a few courses here and there, and, gosh, they keep meaning to get some training courses off the ground, but...

If you are serious, and have go-getter qualities, surf the net yourself, jot down the names of these firms, and propose yourself as an SAP education maestro. This is tantamount to putting a fat worm on a sharp hook and trolling the shallow SAP waters. If you can follow up, you will land some serious business.

In most technical fields, the end-user trainer brings up the rear of the pay scale, and such is true for SAP trainers as well. Unfortunately, you get what you pay for, and more than one implementation has stalled due to a company's desire to save expenses in this crucial area.

As a general rule, trainers seem to make between $40-75 per hour on contract, between $80-120K for module trainers, and between $35K and $60K for end-user trainers, with the high-end reserved for project managers and trainers with multi-year experience.

Most full-time SAP trainers are light on SAP technical experience. It is generally hard to persuade someone with hands-on implementation skills to accept a full-time training position because the salary potential is just not the same. And for the most part, it is not necessary to understand all the inner workings to train end-users (although this knowledge surely is needed). SAP trainers may be the most 'trainable' of all SAP professionals. The old cliché that you can't teach someone how to teach tends to apply.

Companies are sometimes willing to train SAP trainers who have a proven background working with end-users in other comparable software areas, or who have outstanding communication skills or teaching skills. It takes a special patience and very strong communication skills to train effectively, and companies recognize this as they evaluate applicants. Personal interviews become even more important, and the technical phone screen that can be a stumbling block for SAP technical positions is rarely the key factor in SAP training hires, although it is still important.

In terms of the market for end-user trainers, there is a real demand for good trainers; sometimes in early stages of implementations, sometimes in later stages. Training can be an excellent way of getting into SAP, but if your final goal is to move into technical implementation work you may find training to be a dead end. It simply is not enough to prepare you for hands-on implementation work.

Some trainers are jealous of their better-paid technical peers, and are angling to get into that type of work. But it is not always easy to make that transition. Trainers typically have a different, less technical background, and they are often passed over in favor of those who have already handled a technical SAP role. The leading training companies do not have many technical openings to groom you for. The best bet for a trainer who wants to move into configuration work is an all-purpose consulting firm that might cross-train you over time.

The Challenges of a Career in SAP Education

As Patti Walsh puts it. "Trainers are 'on' all the time, whereas consultants have the luxury of saying 'let me get back to you about that.' Instructors have to be entertainers trained in the art of reading body language. They must keep their students attention, even with the most dry subject matter."

Being 'on' all the time with subject matter (SAP) that can very often be very dry, can be fatiguing and that fatigue is coupled with the fact that instructors have to constantly keep up with an ever-evolving product. (Note: in the past three years, R/3 has moved from version 2.2 through to 4.0 with roughly sixteen separate new releases.)

Further, not all course attendees have the same motivation. Some are desperate to soak up SAP knowledge, but others are merely going through the motions with a sense that their career value will rise through the reception of a certificate.

Adds Patti Walsh, "Some students feel they need to prove themselves by finding fault with the teachers, the 'I know something you don't know' syndrome. This is especially prevalent with consultants who take classes with their clients. But who taught the consultants to begin with? Trainers!"

Some trainers prefer the amount of dynamic interaction that a training role provides. They prefer working with people to manipulating data and information. Imagine! These are the people who will be the most successful in the training area in the long run. Companies who have a stable of these types of training consultants are finding that there is plenty of work out there.

If you hear scuttlebutt about an implementation that is on the rocks, you might try to get in touch with the powers that reign over that implementation. Those Fortune 500 projects have a tendency to start, huff and puff, chug, choke, and stop. There is an interval during which education is at last given its due, and trainers are sought at a premium. Then, once a major effort at SAP education has been accomplished, the implementation starts over again, on a proper footing.

Training may not mean the same high-end dollar that you can earn in a technical role, but in the broader view an ambitious, can-do attitude towards your particular SAP niche is probably the most important factor in your long-term success. If training is your niche, go to it. Besides, anything related to SAP tends to bring the pay up beyond subsistence level. If you are not far enough beyond subsistence, consider contracting or working towards a project lead role.

The old saw is that those who cannot do, teach. This is bullroar, and should be retired as a useless cliché.

There is, sadly, a new cliché, and one that is cliché because of its truth:

> *Those who have done and can teach SAP should be paid as much or more than when they are doing, but will not be.*

In the world of SAP, those who can teach and teach well are worth gold, most especially to the students in their classes. So many people wish to receive an SAP education and when they come upon a good, wise, worthwhile instructor, they are more grateful than words can express. This is the true gold of SAP education: the guru status that is yours if you pass the baton with elan.

Says Patti Walsh, "Training is a process not an event. One class does not make an expert. True knowledge is gained over time with lots of practice."

Seek only money in SAP education and you will be disappointed. Seek a combination of solid salary and very high job satisfaction, and that grass is green green green.

Part III:

Managing Your SAP Career

Consulting Rates: Ebb and Flow

Paranoia about falling rates is the classic preoccupation of all SAP consultants as well as those aspiring to this field. As of this writing, the U.S. market outlook remains favorable in the foreseeable future. But the SAP hiring market is complex, and deserves a lengthier analysis.

The key thing to remember is that the SAP hiring market is not like the stock market. Rates will not fall drastically overnight. Careful observation of the market will give plenty of warning signs. If you keep an eye on various Internet

	Demand	Supply	%
1993	2000	500	25%
1995	8000	4000	50%
1997	12000	8000	67%
1999	20000	15000	75%
2001	28000	21000	75%

Skilled SAP *Business* Consultants

sites and job posting boards, you should be able to anticipate precisely which areas of the market are slipping and upgrade your skills accordingly.

The mathematics of rates seems simple: they will stay up as long as demand is high and supply is low. While it is possible to estimate the changes in supply of consultants, demand is a more uncertain variable. If we restrict our focus to the U.S. market, the two factors that should most effect demand are SAP's midsize market focus and the decisions of a smaller group of massive companies who may move to R/3 as a way of addressing year 2000 and related issues.

Clearly, the supply of consultants will continue to go up with each passing year, and the depth of experience of the SAP consultant base will also increase. Unfortunately, it is always difficult to project demand beyond a two-year horizon. Negative factors such as the saturation of Fortune 500 firms are balanced by positives such as SAP's invasion of the mid-sized market and the second wave of implementations within the Fortune 500 world. Large firms that struggled to implement core applications in the mid 90's are now rolling into more exotic efforts such as Workflow, advanced EDI, Internet applications, and the like.

Further, SAP AG and its subset, SAP America, continue to grow at ridiculous rates. 1998 saw another 50% increase in revenues over 1997. We can guarantee you that there were not 50% more SAP consultants in the field over the same period.

What consultants have to take into account is that the demand for quality SAP consulting will remain high while acceptance of standard SAP consultants will fall. By 'standard', we are referring to people with knowledge of SAP but who lack business-specific or industry-specific background. Firms are more and more enticed by consultants with background in specific areas, such as retail or health care, which can be leveraged with some SAP experience. Anyone who can mix in solid consulting skills with these other two elements will have an open playing field for years to come.

Taking a long view, it is pointing out the obvious to say that SAP rates should eventually come down to earth, in line with IS-related pay scales. However, since SAP consulting embraces far more than IS, the rates should remain somewhat higher for years to come. Quality SAP consultants are also 'business consultants' and, as such, will command business rates.

For the majority of consultants, the rates will decline gradually. The good news is that there is a big difference between lowering your rate and being out of work. For those who simply end up with humbler hourly rates, all we can say is, wasn't that fun? And if your rate has fallen from $150 to $135 an hour, who is going to feel your pain?

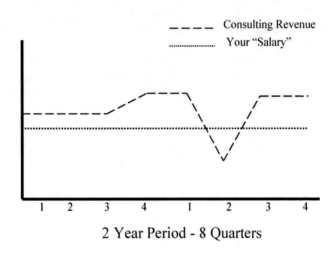

2 Year Period - 8 Quarters

While we are on the subject, independents should be on guard against expectations of continuous, uninterrupted billing. Downtime is zero-income time for you, and yet we observe that great numbers of independents get locked into living on the entirety of their billings and then get caught short when natural down time occurs. These people are often desperate for a new assignment, any assignment, just to keep the cash flow going.

It is wise to maintain a reserve by giving yourself a "salary" equivalent to 80% of your average net (after tax) revenues over a two year period. Having all that cash during your peak billing periods is great, but you will need something to fill the valleys all the same.

A more serious concern is the possibility of large numbers of consultants who might become obsolete in terms of marketable skills. It is possible that some consultants truly are "on the bubble" and when demand catches up they may have no place outside of SAP to go.

We sincerely doubt that large chunks of the SAP consulting market will hit the unemployment lines in any area. One seldom-mentioned factor in the rise of SAP is the relative health of the western economy, most particularly in North America. Projects as massive as SAP endeavors are less enticing when the economy is sluggish. When the pinch comes, it is more likely to be a collective belt-tightening than a frenzy of pink slips. Nevertheless, functional consultants need to understand what their eventual difficulties might be and plan accordingly.

Perhaps the most vulnerable profile is the college graduate, now a Big Five consultant, with one to three years of SAP functional skills and no other relevant experience. For those who are willing to travel and are committed to further training, there should be ample time to retool skill sets before a consulting firm would consider letting you go.

Consulting firms are a great source of career transitioning for those who are up to the continued travel. Perhaps more vulnerable is the SAP functional contractor three years out of school with no company to count on for retraining. But the bulwark against this possibility is in the money that is wisely saved. As long as you set aside funds for a period of job searching and self-financed retraining, you should be able to avoid a disaster.

Consider the same three-years-out-of-school FI configurator who has taken a job at an end-user site. Perhaps this is a vulnerable profile. After all, the IS department may question your technical background, and the finance and accounting managers may wonder about your lack of financial industry experience. But if you recognize now that you might someday face this situation, you can take some appropriate steps to continue your training and anticipate these market shifts.

The other SAP consultant who might face difficulty down the line is the functional specialist with mostly IS background: the programmer who is now a functional consultant (the functional consultant-turned-programmer could also face challenges, but this is a less common situation). The big consulting firms clearly favor the functional consultant with the business process background, such as the FI configurator with an MBA and an accounting background. End-users generally favor the functional specialist with the IS background if they do hire this profile on salary, but once configuration is complete, where does this functional specialist who used to be a programmer wind up?

As a general rule, we believe you should stick to your guns in a particular skill area, so that your resume has a continuity before and after your SAP career. Switch from functional to technical only if you see this as a long term career shift, not a short-term money-maker. Focus on the aspect of SAP that complements your advanced degrees and business or technical expertise. This practical approach will help give you an overall body of expertise that will be appealing whether or not you are dealing with SAP or a different product in the future.

Consultant Compensation Forecast

The following table provides a thumbnail view of the total compensation (salary + bonus) that SAP consultants in firms might expect. The key variables we consider are number of years of industry experience and number of years of SAP experience. The compensation amounts are not fixed in stone. Indeed, about ten percent of the SAP consultants will scratch their heads, wondering why their compensation is so much lower than their coordinate on this table. Another ten percent will laugh (with a certain amount of satisfaction) at how low our figures are.

Compensation Table – SAP Module Implementation Consultant

Years of SAP Experience	Years of Industry Experience			
	1-2	3-4	4-5	5>
<1	$60K-$70K	$60-$70	$60K-$70K	$70K-$90K
1	60-80	60-80	60-80	75-100
2	75-90	75-90	75-90	100-140
3	90-110	90-130	90-140	100-180
4>	90-115	90-140	100-140	110-200

The market is not the same for all module consultants, however, and you can fine-tune your estimate with these variants.

Variant	1999	2000	2001
FI	-$10K	-$15K	-$15K
SD	+10	+10	+15
MM	Even	Even	Even
SD-MM	+10	+15	+15
MM-PP	+10	+10	Even
PP	Even	Even	Even
HR	+10	+10	+10
ASAP Cert.	+5	+5	+5
Mod Cert.	+10	+10	+10
Back Office	+10	+15	+15

An SD consultant with three years of SAP experience on top of three years of industry experience can expect a total compensation between $90K and $130K. By adding ASAP certification and SAP Certification in SD, that consultant can raise the bar to between $105K and $145K.

Contractor rates will follow varying paths depending upon the module practiced and the source of the contract. The figures below are gross rates, meaning what clients will pay for contractor services.

Net amounts received by contractors depend upon the commission taken by body shoppers or other consulting agents.

Contractor Rates

Years of SAP Experience	Years of Industry Experience			
	1-2	3-4	4-5	5>
<1	$60-$100	$60-$100	$70-$100	$70-$100
1	60-100	60-100	60-110	75-120
2	85-120	85-140	90-150	100-160
3	90-150	90-150	100-150	100-160
4>	100-150	100-150	100-175	110-175

Fine tune your contracting estimates with these rates per hour variants:

Variant	1999	2000	2001
FI	-$10	-$15	-$15
SD	+10	+10	+10
MM	Even	Even	Even
SD-MM	+10	+15	+15
MM-PP	+10	+10	Even
PP	Even	Even	Even
HR	+10	+15	+10
ASAP Cert.	+5	+5	+5
Mod Cert.	+10	+10	+10
Back Office	+10	+15	+15
ABAP	-30	-35	-35

An SD contractor consultant with three years of SAP experience on top of three years of industry experience can expect a gross hourly rate between $90 and $150. By adding ASAP certification and SAP Certification in SD, that consultant can raise the bar to between $105 and $165 per hour.

Rates and compensation vary from region to region, but so do tax rates. If you are working in northern California, you will probably make 10% to 15% more than if you were in South Dakota, but you will pay far more in taxes.

More to the point, SAP license saturation in the Northeast and, to some extent, in the South, have already begun to depress rates and compensation, and you may want to drop your estimates in those areas by as much as 15%.

Betty Costa of Grant Thornton has worked in the Big Five, as an independent contractor, and in the mid-sized consulting market. She points out that **"Project management** is in the highest demand and has historically been the lowest in supply (particularly in the mid-sized market)."

We concur, and project that employee remuneration for project managers will rise from the $140K to $220K range to $160K to $260K through 2000. Hourly rates for independents will rise accordingly from a current level of around $200.

Handicapping by Module

Never bet on a horse named Toldyouso and remember that many visionaries are delusionaries. All the same, here is a brief tout sheet for your module to module future.

FI is good, but **FI/CO** is much better. CO is the sexy stuff, the more analytical of the two, the more strategic. Both modules together have a nice future with SAP continuing to dominate the "core apps" market of FI, HR, and manufacturing execution. CO generally has several different sub-modules, and it can be hard to master all of them. CO-PA and CO-PC seem to be the two biggies that you want some exposure in. Note: rarely is it paying off to be focused in more than two related modules, although some additional integration knowledge between your core module expertise and other modules is highly useful.

In essence, FI alone does not offer a northward cash path and would best be combined with CO.

SD-MM has a great outlook, a little more vanilla and lower rates than FI/CO at the start of 1999. However, with the post-Y2K push to the extended supply chain, SD and MM are right along the core of the internal supply chain and the SD/MM logistics consultant is in a great position to capitalize on this. We would rather see SD than MM, but both are better than one. On the SD side, you really want the sales and the distribution portion. These folks are in a great position to eventually get involved in SAP's SCOPE (Supply Chain Optimization, Planning, and Execution) and also to get into the sales force automation stuff that's coming up.

HR offers a focus right now, due to high rates, but all HR folks should get the payroll, benefits, and generally the PA side of the module down. SAP's continued push into "core apps" areas, where clients are going for one integrated solution over a "best of breed" approach, bodes well for HR.. Be a little wary, as the HR area seems to require less overall industry background, giving you little protection from an incoming flock of HR configuration experts. Some of the most promising areas of HR are in the Internet area, with SAP's Employee Self-Service (ESS) functionality being a necessary focus for any forward-thinking SAP HR consultant. It is hard, however, to combine an HR focus with another module. However, there are some nice cross-application HR areas that you can focus on to give you broader exposure, such as CATS (cross application time sheets).

PS is not a commonly used module and one that may not fare as well in the industry-specific, best-of-breed approach that's going to rule the buying and implementation decisions in the non-core areas. However, it can be a good focus to have right now, as long as you combine it with a more mainstream module. The best strategy for those who have "niche module" exposure is indeed to combine that expertise with the one core module most closely related. With some, there are several core modules that might apply. In the case of PS, the FI module is the most common combo. The PS-FI consultant looks stronger towards the future than the PS consultant. Two niche modules should not be combined as a focus, such as PS-PM. This limits marketability.

PM is not as commonly used, and may be in more jeopardy than any other niche module, as industry-specific apps could chip away at the PM appeal. Best used in combination with other manufacturing-related areas, such as PM-MM.

PP This module is more common than PS, PM, or QM now but in the long run could really be trounced by cutting-edge planning and scheduling software, including SAP's own APO release. PP folks want to move into the MM/PP focus as soon as possible, as MM has a better projected life-span.

MM is best applied in conjunction with SD, which amounts to a "logistics" focus, ideal for those with extensive manufacturing backgrounds. MM also works in combination with PP, but SD is the better partner module for the future. It is best not to focus only on MM.

QM is a niche module, but one that may stand the test of time, especially for those with solid quality management industry backgrounds. More companies may turn to QM to optimize their implementation, so it could have a nice life span after all. Or it could end up like Workflow, a good idea that few take advantage of. QM is best, however, in conjunction with a core module, such as MM/QM.

WF. SAP needs to continue to enhance Workflow functionality, and companies need to take the functionality more seriously. This is not a great area to focus on, but nice to have in the "tool chest" along with other integration and connectivity technologies such as ALE and EDI.

AM. Assets Management needs to be combined with an FI focus. This goes for any lingering Treasury and Cash Management folks as well.

The Heat of SAP HR

It should be noted that rates for SAP HR are high because of simple supply and demand. HR was a latecomer to the North American applications suite and did not appear until mid 1996. (North American payroll, benefits, and HR legislation vary greatly from European norms and SAP was slow to complete development of North American HR). Also, SAP HR is not an area that really benefits from deep industry experience in HR payroll systems (as compared with FI/CO, where a deep accounting and finance background can be a major plus). Further, unlike other areas of SAP, the U.S. implementations cannot turn to Europe for SAP HR experience in the North American payroll area. The bottom line is that very few people have more than a year or two of experience in any part of the HR implementation cycle in this particular payroll area.

However, once more people get experience in HR payroll, we see rates declining as the HR area takes its place in the SAP "back office." Companies do not want to spend this kind of money implementing HR systems. They want to spend money on data warehousing, electronic commerce, supply chain optimization, and all those other "extended ERP," "post-Y2K" areas. Therefore, we see the SAP HR market as temporarily inflated, and when it levels off, it should stay leveled off, probably a bit lower than FI/CO in the long run, when all the mission-critical complexities of the CO module are taken into account.

Mmmbop ABAP

One irony is that the current market favors these same functional consultants who may face employment difficulties down the line, whereas the ABAPers and to some degree Basis experts may be the first to feel the crunch. You must plan for the long-term demand and not be blinded by the current superiority of your hourly rate.

ABAP/4 programmers and Basis specialists have a different set of concerns right now. ABAP/4 rates have already started to fall, particularly for your basic ABAP/4 programmer. For this reason, it may even make sense to take a lower rate if you are going to obtain a better quality of experience. The ABAP/4 contractor may have to settle for a rate of $100 or even less, but the ABAP/4-ALE-EDI specialist can still pick up $150 an hour. Keep adding to your basic skill area and make sure you take projects on company sites that are committed to constant upgrades and product enhancements.

The long term forecast for ABAP/4 programmers may be most affected by the evolution of R/3. Each new release from here on out should downplay ABAP/4 in favor of object-oriented enhancements and revisions. This will be a gradual process, however, and the typical ABAP/4 programmer has a strong technical background that should keep the IS career chugging along, albeit at a somewhat reduced rate.

A more promising field of ABAP play is in the burgeoning bolt-on market for SAP. Since 1997, SAP has created dozens of alliances with technical firms for the development of industry-specific bolt-ons, implementation accelerators, and the like. These alliances have virtually doubled SAP's capacity to evolve since they are no longer dependent solely on their own R&D for product enhancement.

Working for one of these firms may take you out of the direct SAP career path since the balance of your experience will be IS related and you will not be gaining implementation project experience. Still, if you feel that software engineering rather than business consulting is more up your alley, you might strongly consider checking out these firms.

Many of these firms are somewhat like Silicon Valley operations in which stock options, equity, and the like may come into play. One downside may be that SAP can always come along with its million munchkin R&D machine and replicate these firms' products into oncoming versions of R/3.

Check out the back of this book for a partial list of technical partners.

George Zatulovsky is co-founder and president of 5th Street Solutions, a consulting and resource placement firm. George has been involved in SAP consulting for the last five years and agreed to offer his experienced insight into the forecast for ABAP. Basis, and outsourcing.

ABAP/4

I absolutely agree that with SAP's object oriented code and JAVA approach, ABAP skills will become less and less popular. There are a lot of JAVA programmers out there! Simple "coders" will not be in demand anymore. They will have to be business-oriented folks, with the ability to design functional specifications and then to code based on those specs.

Communication and business skills are the absolute MUST for the ABAPers. Those are the skills that "offshorers" mostly do not have.

As SAP moves into mid-market companies with limited implementation budget and resources, not only BPR activities, but also extensive bolt-ons and interfaces will become unpopular as these companies most likely will adopt a "vanilla" software. This prediction looks even more likely to happen if you consider relatively recent announcement of SAP's 16 (or 18) Solution Maps, which address unique industry functionality and specific business processes for vertical industries. Basically, you would be able to buy an industry-specific SAP software, with mostly preconfigured business processes (templates), and a light customization ("tweaking") would get you "going live".

With this in mind, more companies will consider the outsourcing for the maintenance activities.

Basis

Similarly, I do not anticipate a huge demand in Basis resources. Some reasons :

The R/3 Simplification Group that develops tools and techniques to make R/3 implementations quicker, cheaper, and easier to understand. Basically, these guys are creating "cookbooks" for almost every aspect of R/3 administration (system installation, authorization profile maintenance, user administration, system landscape, etc). And they have created even more so called "implementation accelerators" for multiple functional modules.

RRR (Ready-to-Run R/3) program that is designed for small-to mid-sized enterprises, It complements the AcceleratedSAP program by combining bundled server and network hardware systems with a pre-installed, pre-configured base R/3 System, operating system, and database.

Outsourcing phenomena

Again, due to the limited budget and resources, small to mid-sized companies may be inclined to outsource at least their R/3 technical support/maintenance activities. This effort (outsourcing) is being simplified by performance monitoring tools introduced by several software vendors (Envive, Luminate Software, OptiSystems, etc.) These tools successfully complement (or should I say compete) with the SAP-native CCMS.

BASIS is Eternal

The Basis contractor is in an interesting situation. Conditions seem to favor the hiring of in-house Basis expertise on salary, particularly for projects in maintenance mode. On the other hand, there are not so many Basis experts who are willing to go on salary, so companies are grudgingly proceeding with Basis contract hires and should be forced to do so for some time come.

The rise in outsourcing will clearly shift the playing field for Basis experts. There will be less demand for their services in the small and mid-sized markets but the outsourcing firms will be offering new challenges and roles.

On the other hand, with the wide range of technical innovations that the typical Basis consultant is exposed to, this may be the area of SAP with the most promising future. The Basis guru is versed in so many crucial IS areas, including relational database administration, systems and network administration, client/server architectural issues, Internet and Intranet connectivity, and security and authorization technologies.

Having a breadth of Basis-related skills is becoming a career must.

All Disciplines

The common denominator that all SAP professionals now face closer scrutiny and strict technical expectations. It is no longer feasible to receive an SAP offer letter on your fax machine without at least a technical phone interview. Every professional in the market is accountable for their experience now, and a track record of proven SAP successes (along with continued training and the pursuit of quality experience over dollars) should provide a high degree of job security for many years to come.

It is this strict premium on experience that is having a ripple on those trying to break into SAP. The market will no longer welcome you with open arms just because you have taken a training class. It may seem odd, if the demand is so high. But companies figure they can pay for their own employees to go through the training if necessary. What they really want is the profile that's still hard to find: the real expert, competent, easy to work with, level-headed, with genuine knowledge of multiple implementations. Enter the SAP market by all means, but understand what you are dealing with and strategize accordingly.

Finally, remember that these are only predictions. The market is volatile, and perspectives differ. We feel we have a good view of the horizon for 1999 through 2001, but are aware that the good people at Apple once thought the same thing.

Caution, S-Curve Ahead

SAP AG was founded on a bedrock principle that it would remain a product-based firm, not a conglomerate of product, services, maintenance, platform supports, and the rest.

However, since the advent of "Team SAP" in the summer of 1997, the supplier takes a direct hand in all implementations and has aggressively built its own consulting force. Parallel to this, SAP has pushed and shoved against the very need for consulting, as if wishing to eliminate consulting from the business equation. Outsourcing, off-the-shelf Accelerated Solutions™, and remote configuration services are meant to reduce client dependence upon consultants and hasten implementation.

The total elimination of consultants will never happen, of course. SAP cannot have it both ways: enterprise-wide do-it-all software on a plug in basis will not appear on the near horizon and even the Accelerated Solutions Lone Ranger concept will not succeed without some SAP-savvy Tontos in the field.

Still, SAP's ongoing efforts to reduce the need for consultants will take effect in small, but telling, ways. SAP education is becoming more and more automated and more and more useful, thus greasing the rails for an easier transfer of SAP knowledge from consultants (or SAP itself) to clients. In the main, this is to the good. We have seen enough clients addicted to greedy consultants and a transfer of knowledge is the greatest service a consultant can provide. Still, the net effect will be less consulting per client endeavor, thus narrowing the market perceptibly.

Our advice to you is to embrace any such initiatives, because success with a client breeds new business, whereas failure breeds only temporary billing.

Enhancing Your Market Value

SAP and Business Process Reengineering

There is a skeptical theory that business process reengineering is a buzz word with no substantive meaning. To some, the phrase is just another over-hyped method of retooling business systems, and too often used as a fancy justification for ruthless layoffs and downsizing. But the reality is that business process reengineering, at its best, is an effective means of improving business performance, a necessary step for competition in a global economy. SAP technology supports business process reengineering. Indeed, an SAP R/3 implementation generally inspires a company to reengineer to some degree.

The advantages of reengineering in all areas, from manufacturing to customer service, would be mostly theoretical without technical innovation.

Enterprise software has become an important part of reengineering efforts, due to the obvious benefits of abandoning what is often a hodge-podge of outdated software utilities in favor of one integrated package. But SAP may be unique in the way that it literally forces a company's hand into a reengineering mode. It is impossible to simply perform a purely technical implementation of the SAP system. In the case of the most efficient, shortest implementations you might hear whispers such as "How did they do that in only three months". What they did was probably a quick implementation of core functions and the remainder of the project is still to follow.

In every SAP implementation, many job descriptions are going to change, and resistance to change is a natural response until the benefits are made clear. If key players in IS and management are not on the same page, an already complex implementation will bog down. Sometimes you will hear about an SAP implementation that has taken months longer than anticipated without achieving basic functional goals. There are a number of reasons why an implementation can stumble, but there are times when SAP gets unfairly scape-goated for internal divisions and leadership problems. SAP's tight controls can bring these problems out in the open, but it rarely causes them.

SAP implementation specialists who focus on the entire life cycle, from the initial 'as is' assessment forward, are familiar with the many organizational challenges involved. Some SAP consultants are more comfortable in a technical role, and are content to leave the 'reengineering' questions to others. Other consultants are skilled at guiding companies through these questions, although it is generally tricky for an outsider to accomplish much without a internal team that is composed of key managers advocating the benefits of the R/3 system.

Before SAP R/3 can be installed, at least some analysis of a company's business practices must be undertaken. This 'as is' phase will be followed by a more thorough 'to be' phase. At this point, while the implementation is still in the early planning stages, it should become obvious how much or how little reorganization will be involved during an installation. Companies who do not undertake a thorough analysis at this point do so at their own peril. In some cases, a careful, 'on-paper' analysis leads companies to realize that SAP is not the right corporate decision for them.

SAP does have the most thorough functionality of any enterprise software program, but it does require users to conform to its specific "best business practices." For example, companies with unusual ways of processing receivables will find out during the planning phase whether or not SAP can support their way of business. It is costly and problematic to rewrite SAP's source code. Sometimes there is a clever way around the glitch, sometimes companies decide to change a practice to adhere to R/3, and sometimes they find an outside vendor with a bolt-on application that will do the trick. In some cases, clients make the decision to live without a minor function because it is simply not significant compared with the many benefits of the system.

Because companies must chart out the most minute detail of how they do business and determine how and if these functions will transfer into SAP, any sloppy loopholes in business practices will be brought into the open. If a company is not prepared to take whatever steps are necessary to address these loopholes, there are going to be problems later on.

What do you say to the current payroll manager whose job calculating benefits will be automated by the R/3 system? And what of the customer service users who, through the use of R/3, will now be able (and required) to answer questions about product availability from plants across the world, who previously handled their own inventory and responded only on a daily basis to sales orders? Unfortunately, without solid cross-department leadership and communication, turf wars and resistance to the changes involved in SAP may be debilitating. The phrase that encompasses the leadership and attitude necessary for these changes is reengineering. Call it what you like, it is taking place on most SAP installation sites.

For some companies, there will be major changes when SAP goes in. For those firms who are already in a client-server environment, with a series of reorganization efforts already completed, the 'reengineering' may feel more like a routine tune-up.

Even those of you who to prefer to focus on the technical side of SAP implementations will find the need for communication skills. This is a reflection of the intense human/end-user factor involved in an SAP installation. Whether or not they are officially involved in reengineering efforts, those SAP technicians with stronger communications skills go farther than equally capable, but less communications-savvy peers.

For many, the real excitement of an SAP implementation is not in the technical work, but in the process problem-solving that is required to make the technical and financial gains a reality. These are marketable skills in the SAP market, but how you perceive your work - as purely a configurator, or as a broader business process person - is an individual decision. Either way, with a strong hands-on technical background, you will be marketable. If you business knowledge relative to workflow, you will be sought after.

When considering whether or not to accept an assignment on a new project, do not hesitate to ask careful questions about the implementation approach to be adopted. You want to work on sites that reflect your own style and strengths. Some companies will not want to address the reengineering aspects, or will have their own approach that may or may not include your input. A few companies can get away with very little reorganization during an install, but none can get away from configuration-type work, so do not neglect this key area if you are a functional consultant.

How the Business Engineering Workbench and Other Configuring Aids Will Effect the Hiring Market

The greatest threat to the pay scale of SAP consultants may have less to do with competitors' products, and more to do with the streamlining of SAP configuration from within. In 1996, SAP announced the availability of automated configuration tools which may have a major effect on the SAP marketplace. As ComputerWorld has noted, "The new tools...promise to slash millions of dollars from users' implementation costs by reducing the need for high-priced R/3 consultants."

These new tools, called the Business Engineering Workbench (BEW), are SAP's answer to the automatic configuration software now provided by BaaN, one of its main competitors. The BEW tools save labor time during the crucial configuration phase, potentially cutting this time in half. BEW provides a central Business Repository and a vast collection of 800 business processes and 170 core business objects. These objects can be used exactly as they are or they can be configured using graphical tools.

The BEW tools give companies a ready-made framework, ensuring that they will not need to set up their system from scratch. BEW provides a template which minimizes the need for intense customization. The heart of BEW is the R/3 Reference Model, which is a thorough collection of business practices that the user can manipulate and fit to the needs of the company. Perhaps most significantly, BEW allows changes to the system to be made on the go, without the need for cumbersome reprogramming.

Another significant BEW feature is the Open Business Repository API, an open API to the Business Repository which streamlines the interfacing of SAP with external systems. According to SAP, this new API will vastly reduce the need for low-level programming and custom coding of each interface. The API should prove especially useful for integration with legacy-based systems. SAP will license the R/3 Reference Model so that third parties can take advantage of this new ease of integration.

If you are concerned about your value as an SAP consultant in the face of these automated tools, you are not alone. But keep in mind that SAP needs the BEW tools to remain competitive as it seeks out new clients and implementation sites. And no system as complex as SAP can ever be implemented without some human intervention. Obviously, as SAP labor requirements decrease, the supply of consultants will start to catch up with the demand, and your rates could go down. By the same token, new tools offered by SAP which reduce implementation time have helped land hundreds of new accounts amongst the all-important, cost-conscious market of mid-size companies.

Once again, it is always more productive to focus on upgrading your own skills rather than waiting for the market to bring bad news to your doorstep. Clearly, if you specialize in SAP configuration, you may want to study these new tools and determine the areas of SAP implementation where human know-how and expertise will still be in high demand, and make sure your skills include these labor-intensive areas.

For example, there is no way to automate project management, pre-sales, or marketing. Since SAP is often part of a broader process reengineering effort, those who understand and can facilitate this broader process will remain in demand. It is also difficult to imagine automation replacing a Basis consultant.

Consulting Skills

This is merely a consulting career handbook. To succeed in consulting, no matter what level of SAP skills you have to offer, you should possess honed and refined consulting skills or your career will be undermined.

Consulting elements that should be addressed include:

Appearance

Conforming to client dress codes is a minimum requirement. Most highly successful consultants establish their own relatively formal dress code and stick to it no matter what the client requirements may be. It is not necessarily good advice to always try to "fit in" with your client contacts. Distinguishing yourself may be a better idea.

Client Relations

How close should you be to your client contacts? In some cases, familiarity will truly breed contempt. In other cases, bonding will lead to greater success.

Consultants who remain successful for three or more years are often those who learn early on that repeat business is the best business. If you merely skip from job to job, you may widen your network or contacts or burn your bridges depending upon your skill at client relations. Repeat business is usually evidence of a combination of expertise and professionalism.

Your Work Schedule

The hours you work and the location are often prime elements of a client's vision of who you are and what worth you bring. Few client contacts will know exactly what it is you are doing for them, no matter how voluminous and detailed your status reports may be. Some clients want you to be present and on-site at all times; others are more interested in seeing results than your head bowed to a screen.

If you are traveling to and from the client site, you may want to establish a "pyramid" schedule so that you can be home at comfortable (or at least acceptable) hours on weekends. Late Friday arrivals and Sunday evening departures are a strain.

In a "pyramid" schedule, you fly out on Monday mornings and arrive at the client site by noon latest. You may only work five or six hours that day, then work ten hours on the Tues-Thur run, and then four or five on Friday with an early afternoon return home. Few clients object to such a schedule. Those clients who do object will probably pose even more serious problems.

Scope of Work

The best consultants tend to surpass the scope of the work required. They spend an extra hour or two each week adding value to their efforts and such consultants are often rewarded with repeat business.

Working beyond client expectations may seem like a slam dunk, but you have to gauge the limits of what you can do. Some client contacts react badly if you go beyond the established scope, assuming that you have not done what you were supposed to do but instead worked on what you felt like. If this may be the case, remember to first demonstrate that you have fulfilled the identified scope of work, and then present whatever you have done in addition.

In this same light, if your out-of-scope-efforts will result in additional hourly billing, be sure that the client has agreed *in advance* or you may have some embarrassing moments trying to collect.

Language

Clients have an aversion to "consultant-speak" and rightfully deride consultants who use trendy phrases rather than concrete language. "Consultant speak" is, unsurprisingly, most commonly used by consultants straight out of MBA programs, but we have heard our share from older folks who should know better.

Phrases gleaned from journals and books may be introduced into a project context but you will have to measure client tolerance for them. One example is the term "business process reengineering", which has often been confused with downsizing and has just as often been viewed as a consultant's pretext for additional billing. Although any SAP implementation engages a firm in the change of its business processes and the term should therefore be acceptable, you may have to find another label for it.

You will necessarily have to teach your clients a number of SAP terms, and you should do so in a diplomatic fashion. Do not speak over the client's head in an attempt to distinguish yourself; instead, ascertain each individual's comfort zone when it comes to SAP terms and adjust your vocabulary so that you can be understood.

Adds Betty Costa, "You should speak in terms relative to the level you are addressing; end-user to end-user, technical to technical, executive to executive."

Certifications

In the "early days" of SAP consulting (1993-1996), obtaining SAP certification as a consultant was both easy and pointless. During that time, the crying need for SAP consultants made certification a foregone conclusion once you showed up at a partner academy.

All that has changed, however, and obtaining certification in your chosen module is both meaningful and profitable. SAP America has radically improved its certification process and requirements, to such point that consultants who are not certified are finding themselves at a disadvantage.

Betty Costa offers a refinement on this point: "I do not think this is the case in the middle market. Clients still prefer a knowledgeable person who interacts well with a project team to someone who simply has a certification."

A second certification that is growing in importance is the Accelerated SAP certification. The success and popularity of ASAP has led to its adoption by all but the very largest of the SAP practices (i.e. Big Five, IBM, et al). George Zatulovsky points out that ICS/Deloitte and IBM "are I are presenting to the clients a "blended" methodology that has ASAP as a component, together with the firm's proprietary one (i.e., FastTrack from ICS/DT)."

Beyond the certification, your understanding of ASAP will enhance your consulting performance and contribute to your professional portfolio.

Unfortunately, it is nearly impossible for an individual to get certifications without affiliation with an authorized consulting firm. SAP has run some pilot programs for individual certification in ABAP over the years, but general access to certification is restricted to consulting partners and their employees.

To become certified, you must pass the exam for a given course. You do not necessarily have to take the training course itself in order to take the certification exam. If you are working on a end-user site as an employee of an implementing firm, you will have access to SAP training courses through your employer (the exact same courses and course numbers as the actual certification classes), with the caveat that you cannot actually receive the certification if you are an end-user employee. You have to be a member of a consulting partner to actually become certified. This represents SAP's best attempt to train end-users but not blatantly stamp them as "future consultants," which would obviously hurt relations with SAP's install base.

According to an article in *Information Week*,

> ...It would appear that IT managers struggling to recruit and retain staff are in no position to require job candidates to be certified. But a Dataquest study forecasts the demand for certified professionals will grow about 15% annually through

2003, despite the skills shortage. That's because, as IT becomes more central to a company's success, IT managers must be sure the people they hire can deliver.

There are other benefits to certification, according to Diane Tunick-Morello, research director for Gartner Group. Well-trained employees tend to be more effective and more motivated, and they demonstrate a willingness to stay with an organization longer, she says.

Professionals looking to get certified can typically turn to three sources: vendors offering to train people in the use of their products; industry associations that offer vendor-neutral training in a technology area, such as Web-site architecture; and professional training companies that may offer certification for a particular product or in a technology area.

Vendor training is evidence of knowledge of a system, rather than proficiency in it, says Judy Weller, an analyst at Dataquest, while vendor-neutral certification from a training company or industry association provides general skills in a technology area. Recruiters say an IT professional's best bet is to have both vendor-neutral and vendor-specific certifications.

An associate in J.P. Morgan's IT department, who requested anonymity, has found that having certification in Java and C++ from New York University is an advantage. "Certification proves to an employer that you have a certain level of competency," he says. "Anyone can say they know computers, and that's one of the problems today. An employer looks at experience and your college degree. Having certification on your resume can give you an advantage-and possibly a higher salary-than someone without certification. "

And, pounding home a theme we have keynoted in this book (from the same article):

> ...But in addition to technical certification, IT professionals should keep in mind the growing importance of business skills. According to Gartner Group, IT-related skills within a company *will shift from being 65% technology-related today to 65% business- and IT management-related in 2002.* (our italics)

INFORMATIONWEEK -- 10-26-98,
[Copyright 1998, CMP Publications]

Making Your Skills "Recession Proof"

We believe that every SAP career choice, permanent and contract, should be made with "skills enhancement" as THE primary consideration, even taking precedence over rate. It is not necessary to leave the contract market in all cases, but we do advise a shift in focus for contractors, with less attention to "market rate" and more attention to skills.

You want to capitalize on the market, but more importantly, you want to make your skills recession-proof. There are two key ways to do this.

(1) Chase the "Hot" Areas, But Retain Your Core Skills

If you are an ABAP/4 programmer in FI, worried about the potential for declining rates, your first tendency might be to try to become a functional consultant, where the rates seem a bit more promising in the long term. However, we believe that the best choice is not to abandon your core competencies, but *to build upon them.* If you have many years of programming experience, you might not want to make a move to functional consulting in FI or SD or MM. In the long run, you will be competing for engagements with FI consultants who have many years of accounting and finance experience, and perhaps an

MBA to boot. If, on the other hand, you have a strong functional background, and only recently became a programmer in order to break into SAP, then perhaps a switch to functional work is in order.

So what about the ABAP/4 programmer in FI who has a good technical background? How would such a person use this core competency to their advantage? One option could be to get on a project where there will be significant exposure to ABAP programming in the HR module, which has been a growth area for the past few years and promises to remain so. Another would be to take a permanent position with leadership potential, with an eye to becoming a technical lead or project manager. (This is actually our next strategy, and we'll return to it in a moment).

From this vantage point, it seems to us that the best use of this "core competencies" approach is to try to get your skills as close to the "front office" as possible. SD/MM consultants with strong logistics background should be pushing towards increased supply chain management exposure. SD consultants with a sales background might want to pursue areas related to customer management and sales force automation, and to choose projects that focus on integration points between these applications and SAP. In the HR module, there is a great deal of potential in the use of SAP-Internet technologies to enhance HR functionality, such as employee self-service applications. And for ABAP/4 programmers and Basis specialists, integration technologies such as SAP-EDI, ALE, and SAP/BAPI/Internet work could be important considerations when you look at new projects and employment opportunities.

The implications of these "front office" technologies are far-reaching, and instead of giving up on your current skills entirely, it is a better use of your time to figure out how you can get involved in the part of the front office that relates to your particular focus in SAP. Build on your core of skills, but don't abandon them in a wild chase for rate gratification. Whatever your current SAP focus, there is a cutting edge area not too far away.

(2) Use SAP as a Vehicle for Rapid Advancement

If you feel that you have already capitalized on the market financially, then now might be a good time to take advantage of the market power of SAP to vertically advance your career.

The best way to do this is to secure a permanent position of some kind. Two attractive options are a) an equity position in a smaller consulting firm, or b) a "partner track" position in one of the larger consulting firms. (A third option could be a leadership position in IT at an aggressive end-user firm. This particular strategy is based on the theory that your SAP skills can help you to advance up the corporate food chain much faster than the management consultant without "red hot package" experience.)

Because SAP is still a major buzzword in consulting circles, it is a good time to begin this climb. You will need SAP's continued mystique to help you in your advancement. We have seen many consultants take advantage of the market in this way, accelerating themselves into partner positions and cutting down the time it should have taken them dramatically. They may credit their own management talents, but give the "dazzle" of SAP its due as well.

You can also use this strategy as a contractor, albeit with a more limited effect. The ABAP/4-FI contractor we mentioned earlier could use this tactic. Instead of taking the first project that comes along, you could hold out for a team lead role. Keep in mind that many times when you use this "SAP as Vehicle" strategy, you might end up making a lot less money in the short-term, but you stand to reap real long term benefits: job security far into the future. One consultant we talk to calls this "building your professional net worth," as opposed to "cashing in your chips" in the SAP contracting world.

Conclusion

You can make your SAP career recession-proof by aggressively chasing the hot areas that build upon your core skills. If you can also maintain a continuity-of-skills from your previous industry experience into your SAP years, so much the better. Attaching your career prospects to the SAP engine is always a useful tactic, especially in permanent positions, where SAP can really "grease the wheels" and help you to achieve long term professional goals in a shorter time period that you could have hoped for otherwise.

Make sure that you keep yourself in hands-on implementation settings (unless you are advancing beyond project manager). Even project managers needs the hands-on component. Once you move beyond project management, you can reluctantly let go of the hands-on component. In keeping with this approach, it is important to get exposure to the full implementation cycle whenever possible, and to time your departures to coincide with the completion of key phases of the implementation. Avoid maintenance mode whenever possible, unless there are cutting edge "front office" projects on the horizon. Establish yourself on either the technical or functional side of SAP, whichever makes the most sense for your background and goals, and maintain a healthy focus on one side or the other, with perhaps an 80/20 skills divide between functional and technical if possible.

On the technical side of SAP, choose a focus between Basis and ABAP and build upon it, drawing on the "integration technologies" of SAP-EDI, ALE, and Internet as much as possible. Technical SAP folks should do all they can to make "big picture" contributions and to understand the business objectives driving the implementation. In the long term, "back room techies" are not going to thrive in SAP.

On the functional side, make sure that you are getting hands-on implementation skills, including solid configuration skills, hopefully in a module (or two) that relates directly to the functional background of the consultant. Although you MUST have proven configuration skills, there is a real danger in too much focus on configuration, which is a "soft" technical skill, and also a proprietary skill. Whenever possible, get <u>full life cycle implementation experience,</u> including but <u>not limited to the configuration phase.</u> When doing configuration, focus on the interaction with the client, successfully working with them to achieve the functionality that matches the project plan. These are the skills that will be relevant far beyond SAP- these are the skills that will make you truly "recession-proof."

Finally, do not neglect the growing mid-market. If possible, get experience doing ASAP implementations. Certifications are not the ultimate goal here, but obtaining relevant certification from SAP America is the polishing touch on your objectives.

When to Hold 'Em, When to Fold 'Em

Let's Make a Deal!

One SAP consultant writes: "It turns out I made a mistake in my job search. After joining a Big Five firm in February, I am ready to enter the SAP job market again. My experience now includes sixteen months at one Big Five firm, followed by six months at another. I have spent the entire time on SAP projects, and with increasing levels of responsibility. I have received excellent performance evaluations and have solid references, but just haven't found the right career fit yet. What is your opinion of how my "job-hopping" will affect my chances of finding a good position in the current SAP market?"

Even in the fast-moving SAP world, it makes sense to pay careful attention to the amount of job changes you make. Contractors do not have to think as much about the duration of assignments, but if you are committed to working on a salaried basis with a progressive career path, with increasing levels of compensation and responsibility as you advance, you need to time your career transitions carefully.

On the other hand, to stay in a situation that is unsatisfying to you or limiting in its advancement potential does not make sense.

An ancient game show, "Let's Make a Deal" offered the winning contestant a last test, the choice of any of three doors, behind each of which was the equivalent of new car, a trip to Europe, or a pair of used sneakers. Watching these contestants labor over the final decision was usually a hoot, especially when they changed their minds more than once. "Door number one. No, door number two. I mean, no, number one. Oh, Monty!"

Once the choice was made, the host, Monty Hall would first show the contestant what was behind the unchosen doors, leading to either agony or ecstasy, leading right up to "Show them what they've won!"

In the job market, you only get to see what is behind the door you have chosen. Whatever is behind those other doors remains forever a mystery. All the same, since SAP consultants are in a seller's market, the other doors (far more than three altogether) are ever there, tempting you.

To keep the scuff marks off your career shine, you are advised to establish a vision of what you want to do in two and four year increments.

Some job-hopping is not necessarily a negative, as long as you frame it in a sensible manner in your cover letters and interviews.

In some cases, you may need to put a bit of a spin on your reasons for leaving that will make sense to an employer. For example, you may have left your last two positions because of conflicts with supervisors on your management track. Future employers are going to be unreceptive to this reason. "I have had conflicts with my supervisors in my last two positions" is not a winning interview line.

Even reasonable people occasionally run into these dilemmas. A better way of approaching this issue would be to depersonalize it. Frame it in terms of management policies, not personalities. One such example: "I am interested in your firm because you are a performance-based enterprise with rapid opportunities for advancement and few layers of management. My previous firms had rigid structures and many layers of management. Reviews were annual, and I'm looking to make a more immediate contribution."

If you are leaving simply for more money (and otherwise you have no other dissatisfactions with your current position) then you can start by being honest with yourself. You have to consider that you may be damaging your long-term interests by switching too quickly or too often. In the long run, SAP employers are more impressed with those who see their implementations through, and do not switch from job to job so quickly. The SAP world is relatively small, and people who move around too much for financial reasons do get a reputation that follows them. It is true that every time you move you stand a good chance of increasing your salary. But you also run the risk of pricing yourself out of the market.

If you have not completed a project from A to Z, a number of clients will automatically exclude you from consideration. In many cases, this is unfair and myopic. Vast numbers of experienced SAP consultants have labored for years on global projects at places like Bristol Myers Squibb, Hercules, and Lockheed Martin and cannot relate to an interviewer the elation of the post-implementation party.

Some firms are scared away by the high salaries that seem to come with the SAP job-hopper. In the long run, you do better by performing at your current employer and building your reputation as someone who can see projects through and close them out. If your frequent job changes are really about money, then you might want to consider contracting. As a contractor, you can shift projects quickly without doing any harm to your long term career as a contractual employee.

Reasons for a Job Change (Other than $$)

Now that we've taken a look at problematic reasons to make frequent SAP job changes, let's look at some very valid reasons that many SAP job-seekers have expressed. **Travel versus family** or personal concerns is one classic reason for a job change.

Perhaps you were led to believe that you would work on the Left Coast, but you find yourself flying to the Right Coast every week instead and the time away from home is a hardship for you. You have brought this up with your firm and have not received an acceptable response. You can smell the coffee and it is stale. It is time to find a firm with a stronger Left Coast practice.

Professional development is another common reason for a frequent switch. Perhaps upon your hiring, you were led to believe that you would be able to get functional training in SD or certifications, and you have not yet received them despite raising this question with your current employer. You are looking for a firm that will give you that functional opportunity.

Bench time is probably the most persuasive reason of all for a change. Despite the urgent need for SAP consultants throughout the world, some firms are simply poorly organized or unable to sell projects and the result is that sterling SAP talent grows tarnished from sitting around. No matter how much you are getting paid, if you are on the bench for more than a month or so, you might raise your periscope and start scanning the waters. Or, as Betty Costa, advises "Gain some experience in the SAP sales cycle, costing, and approval hoops needed to undertake such an initiative."

(On the subject of bench time, are you simply getting a breather while the game goes on, or are you watching and learning more about how the game is played?)

Another consultant writes: " I have two months of programming experience. How long should I wait before looking into potential opportunities?"

In this consultant's case, it seems that the primary motivation for moving on is taking advantage of the financial perks of the SAP marketplace. Because he/she is still able to gain experience on the job, it is not so much a question of being stifled professionally, and more a question of when to move on to maximize income.

This consultant may have the right tactic in mind. For most SAP professionals, it makes little sense to move on two months into their SAP experience. But for ABAP/4 programmers, there are many more opportunities for light experience than in other areas of SAP. Most folks with two months experience who decide to test the waters are best off looking to the Big Five, where additional training will be provided to supplement the current skills.

A better solution for this consultant may be to deepen and expand his experience on his current job. Since he is in ABAP programming, he might make a point to learn about what decision-making led to the programming he is doing. Is he coding special management reports? If so, why was ABAP chosen to produce them rather than SAPscript or some other tool? What business purpose are the reports intended to fulfill? Are there other means of satisfying the client?

Experience accumulates in direct proportion to what you do *beyond* the base job description you are assigned. You may lag longer than you wish on a given assignment, but there could be gold waiting down the line for you if you take advantage of that lag time to, uh, learn.

"I just got a job offer for $67,000. The bad news is that it's a version 2.2 environment. What should I do?"

To put this query into perspective, you have to understand that version 2.2 was surpassed in 1997 by version 3.0, which has since been surpassed by 3.1 and version 4.0. Therefore, experience on version 2.2 will be of limited value in the market.

Perhaps this consultant's best route is to investigate the 2.2 opportunity and determine how soon an upgrade to 3.1 or 4.0 is planned. Quite possibly, this will be happening with the coming months and the choice will become much easier. However, it may not be worth downgrading skills just to improve upon salary.

The first step towards making the right decision is discarding any paranoia about 'am I making market rates' and take a hard look at your own particular circumstances. In the short-term, the amount of money you are making is rarely as important as the quality of your experience.

As a general rule, you should stick around your implementation site for at least a year if you really want to capitalize on your skills. But this is not always possible, and many people want to make the best of their SAP knowledge while the market is hot.

At this time, it makes sense to have some faith in the mid-term SAP market and resist the cattle-call towards a new position. In this particular consultant's case, a $50K salary, while not extravagant, is not all that bad for six months of experience.

Although it generally makes sense to hold on for a year before moving, this depends on the quality of the SAP experience. Because this contributor is not focusing on SAP full-time, it would make sense to look at either moving on sooner, or looking to expand his/her role in the SAP side of the implementation.

Another key factor, we repeat, is the **length of the implementation cycle.** Making it through a full cycle is *extremely valuable* to the SAP job seeker. Clients and prospective employers tend to ask simple questions like "How many implementations have you completed?" The length of an implementation cycle can vary from four months to four years. For consultants who have worked on global projects, the question is somewhat off the mark and such consultants should be prepared to present their experience in project phases that were completed.

"I am currently involved in an SAP implementation working as a Basis specialist. I have been involved with the project from the start. I have participated in the hardware and database vendor selection process, setup and configuration of the machines, multiple installations and upgrades of R/3, Unix system administration and Oracle database administration for all systems. I also continue to provide Unix systems support, and Oracle DBA administration support to other, non-SAP projects. I have worked with SAP for about a half year and currently make a salary in the 50s. I am not really familiar with the opportunities available or where my skills would fit. Is it best for me to it tight or to start looking?"

There is no right answer to such a question, but one tip is that this consultant has had only six months at SAP. Finishing at least one year would seem to make sense, most especially because of the cachet of coming from SAP itself. If the SAP consulting market is hot in December, it should still be hot the following June. Our advice would be to stick it out.

At this time, it makes sense to have some faith in the short-term SAP market and resist the cattle-call towards a new position. In this particular reader's case, this 50K salary, while not extravagant, is not all that bad for six months of experience. But there may be some cause to move on. For example, a Basis specialist with only 6 months experience can sometimes make a powerful job move on the strength of years of Oracle DBA experience. So this reader's decision would be partially based on the amount of RDBMS background.

For many, the desire to move on is based on your sense that you are underpaid, and eventually that does become a legitimate reason for moving. But even though you are an SAP professional, a player in the IS job market, you should still look at all the factors in a job search. If you are obtaining quality experience at a high-profile client, do not move in haste. Readers are wise to think about and make proactive moves, but be sure that you make a move that addresses your skills as well as your cash flow. And don't let the sense that you are missing out on the big money force you out before your time.

Summary

Early in your SAP career, your focus should be quality of experience, not financial compensation. As the market tightens, those consultants with a proven track record and stellar references are going to have an edge. It is hard to obtain such a track record while hopping from job offer to job offer.

If you are about to complete a key phase of your implementation cycle, or if you are watching outside consultants get the best exposure while you clean up after them, then it may indeed be time to move on. As a general rule, it is harder to break into the contract market than to obtain a Big Five type permanent position, so this should also be taken into account before you make your move.

Have some faith in the SAP market and don't move based on the panic that you're going to miss out. Bide your time, and make your move decisively when your skills are at their peak. Yes, you could miss out on the gravy train. But the best consultants have a real savvy for when to compromise on dollars for skills and when to focus on compensation. You will need to maintain a concern for both throughout your career. As a rule, however, implement now, and cash in later.

Balancing and Measuring Multiple Offers

There is Nearly Always More Than One Offer

Some years ago, Jody Reed was the second baseman for the Los Angeles Dodgers. Having played well for them for the previous two years, he turned down an offer to play for three more years for in excess of six million dollars. Instead, he chose to test the free agent market and proceeded to wander from one negotiation to another. He finally signed a one-year contract with the San Diego Padres for the princely sum of $500,000 and did not top this mark in the following two years. One miscalculation: nearly five million simoleons down the drain.

Although SAP consulting can be lucrative, the numbers do not match major league baseball. Still, clumsy balancing of job or contract offers can cost you money and lay a few body blows to your reputation.

"I have a good job offer from PriceWaterhouseCoopers, but I've also been speaking with ICS Deloitte. I don't want to burn bridges with PWC, but I want to have another option to compare. What should I do?"

It is better to take a direct approach than to do an end-run around one company to keep things alive with another. In the SAP consulting world, your reputation stays with you. Consultants have turned down offers only to realize six months later that they made a mistake. If you handle yourself with class during the hiring process, you should be able to revisit these opportunities again.

We once witnessed a vivid example of this principle in action, involving an SAP consultant who turned down an offer from a Big Five firm, opting instead to remain with his current company under the pressures of a counter-offer. Three weeks later, he decided he had made a mistake. Because he had been straightforward in his negotiations and made pains to maintain a good relationship with the new firm, he was able to revisit, the offer was extended to him a second time, and he accepted.

The golden rule is to conduct yourself just as you would if you were already working for the other firm. Deal directly and responsibly with your contact person, be specific about your timeline, and they will almost always respect you. Perhaps this sounds like common sense, but in the stress of the hiring process it is easy to burn bridges as you attempt to keep your options open.

Some consultants in your situation will go ahead and accept the offer on the table, continue to interview with other companies, and potentially take another company's offer instead, even after the previous company's start date is set and they are expecting you. As a general rule, companies will put up with the ups and downs of the SAP hiring process, but they consider offer acceptance to be a formal commitment, not a bargaining chip or an opportunity for a consultant to keep one door open while exploring another.

Playing for Time

Because the stakes are high for all parties, the most effective approach is to be direct, yet careful. For example, it never pays to tell a company that you cannot accept their offer because you are looking at five or six other situations, or because you are trying to get the maximum amount of money out of the market. Even if you are simply working every possible angle, simply ask for more time. If you can, be specific about how much more time you need, and do your utmost to stick with that timetable.

The deadlines companies attach to offers can be extended in some cases. Most companies understand that SAP professionals are going to want to weigh out their options. After all, if you are not a good fit with this company, chances are you'll move on again in six months or less, not a winning experience for either party. Usually a company will allow a consultant another week to decide on an offer, as long as they are notified in advance. It is much better to mention your other option early on; companies get nervous about dark horses that appear late in the process.

Given the difficulties of putting an SAP team together, clients are often under the gun to get someone quickly. This leads to the hurry-up-and-wait syndrome that is endemic to the market. A project is scheduled to start in two weeks and the client still has not found an SD-MM specialist. The word goes out and resumes flood in. While the client is poring over them, someone decides to change the project start date to three months later *but no one passes on the word to the recruiters*. And two and half months later, the crazed race starts all over again.

In other cases, the client may be more leisurely but that still does not give you all the leash you may need. If you postpone an offer repeatedly, the company may opt to rescind it, although this happens less often than people think. It makes sense to weigh out your hiring options, but it does not make sense to keep putting off a good offer while waiting endlessly for a better one. This may also be the tip that, in your heart, you do not want to pursue the offer you already have.

Economics, Ethics, and Trashed Nerves

The SAP hiring market exerts a particular pressure on all parties. Everybody makes mistakes while interviewing under these circumstances. But if you keep your dealing aboveboard, and seek appropriate counsel when you face a tough judgment call, you will not regret the effort you put into your maintaining your professional reputation. At some point the SAP market will settle down, and you will be glad that you took the time to solidify your base of contacts. Right now, you have the upper hand with companies, and they will remember how you play your cards.

You should also be aware that the world of SAP is still small enough so that what goes around *will* come around. Further, if you are constantly entertaining new and multiple offers, you will be going around a lot faster than if you have a stable career.

The following behavioral patterns enrage clients, recruiters, and consultants alike:

The Butterfly, who moves from job to job, usually in three to five month increments, never completing an assignment because new and seemingly sweeter deals just keep coming along.

The Perpetual Negotiator, who agrees to a list of conditions, but continues to renegotiate throughout an assignment.

The Fabricator, who carpenters a resume and bluffs through the interview process but, once in the field, proves to be useless. (Fabricating is often viewed as a sleight-of-hand way to gain valuable experience; if you are not kicked off a project until after three months or so have passed, hey, you just got three whole months of experience. You will still have left a great professional stain on your name and it will cost you down the line.)

The Time Bomb starts out the interview process as the most agreeable, reasonable consultant, but once the client puts an offer together, this individual suddenly morphs into an aggressive and high maintenance consultant, with all kinds of requirements (big and small) that surface before the deal can be agreed upon. Items that were never mentioned initially tend to crop up, such as a parking space within 50 feet of the building or a three day, 13 hour work-week. Often the "Time Bomb's" rates go up dramatically at the last minute for no other reason than "it was worth a shot" or "my friend told me I was getting low-balled."

The Mercenary, who is very confident in his/her highly rare "flavor of the day" SAP skill set (e.g. variant configuration, HR-payroll), and uses this uniqueness as a club to drive the rate up during the interview process, knowing there are few alternatives other than to pay up. Although the Mercenary deserves credit for being upfront about his/her rate requirements, once the project actually begins, this 'hired gun' mentality can have a detrimental effect on the project team, the rest of whom are striving mightily to create a team-oriented approach.

The Player, who seems to make a hobby out of collecting job offers. Whether the Player will actually take an offer is an open question (or perhaps the Player will accept several offers at once and show up for work at none of them). Sometimes the highly advanced Player will skillfully play one offer against another, setting up a bidding war for their services. In other cases, the Player is simply gratified by all the attention and ends up accepting one offer and then another with an almost charming innocence. This type of individual is the well-known "bridge burner" who will need to curb these tendencies before the market tightens up. Word *does* get around.

The Wimp (or Whiner), who refuses to understand that when you are being paid better than 90% of those around you, you have to give it an extra effort and 'do what it takes' to get the project done on time. The Wimp is constantly at odds with clients about amount of hours spent on the project and will tend to have a sour face at 'crunch time' when long work weekends and a couple of 'red eye' flights are called for. The Wimp does not mess up a project, but does not leave with a glowing reference either.

The Cookie Cutter is technically competent but has a business vision 'as narrow as a railroad track' (Betty Costa's words). "These folks are limited by the way they have seen the product implemented over and over again and do not look for *a better way*."

Many people could get away with such behavior in the period from 1993-1997. The market was wide open then and clients were so desperate to fill teams that good judgment often was tossed out in favor of dispatch.

With each passing month, firms are tightening up the search process, checking references more scrupulously, and learning to wait until the right resource comes along.

As gratifying as it is to be wanted, and in the world of SAP you will find you are truly *needed*, it is unwise to behave as if you will always be on the throne.

The Finer Points of SAP Contracting

The trend towards SAP contracting is driven by the pervading sense that there is a window of opportunity to take advantage of. All the experts have their own forecast, but we all know that someday SAP rates are going to fall. This line of thinking would imply that you should cash in now, so that you don't run the risk of missing out on the good rates. Sooner or later, every salaried consultant finds out how much they are being billed out for ($175 an hour is a current average). And the natural question becomes, "Why can't I get that rate myself?"

> Wally: I'm thinking of quitting and becoming an entrepreneur. I want to experience life on the edge full of risk and challenge and adventure.
>
> Dilbert: The company stops paying you if you quit.
>
> Wally: Oh, then. Never mind.

Unfortunately, it's not quite that simple. The Big Five consulting firms are in a position to bill out at a much higher rate than you can obtain as an independent. They bill based on "the prestige factor." If you get in as an independent, part of the reason a company wants you is to save some money on rates.

But if you cannot make the rate that you are being billed out at, you can sure get closer. And if you are working for an end-user, you can potentially triple or even quadruple your gross income as a contractor.

Some people are shy about going for the money. There is nothing wrong with taking the chance to "cash in" on your skills. As an SAP professional with experience, you are like a professional athlete. Your chance to capitalize on your skills financially will only last for a finite period of time. This is as close to a get-rich-quick scheme as you are going to find.

When you make decisions about contracting, you should keep these points in mind.

There are few true "independents." Most companies will only hire contractors through a select group of approved vendors. This means that there will always be someone taking a piece of your hourly rate in exchange for connecting you to the project.

The obvious question is then, "How much should I allow a vendor to take?" This is not a line of thinking that will generally lead to good business relationships. A better approach is "How much do I need to make on this project?" If you are happy with your rate, the type of project, the location, and the duration, don't stress out about the cut your vendor is taking. The percentages vary wildly, from 5% of your bill rate to as high as 45%. The reality is that what is fair to you may not be fair to someone else. And your ability to negotiate depends on the amount of projects you have to choose from, your geographical flexibility, your living expenses, etc. Approach each project with your own expectations and if you are in doubt, consult a variety of knowledgeable sources in terms of what your market rate might be.

It is very difficult to contract in the U.S. unless you are a permanent resident or U.S. citizen. This is the result of the timing of projects and the generally immediate need for contractors versus the lengthy process of securing an H-1. If you require an H-1 sponsorship to contract, you can either look for a firm that will hold your visa from project to project, or you can go full time with a company and try to obtain a green card first. We advise obtaining a green card unless you are only planning to stay in the U.S. for a short time.

There are really only two options for contracting, W-2 hourly and incorporated billing. For those who are just entering the contract market, we advise the W-2 arrangement. Typically, this means that the vendor that places you on a project will put you on their payroll as a W-2 employee for the duration of that project. This is a convenient arrangement that allows for you to focus on your SAP project work and not worry as much about your tax responsibilities. Contractors who are in contracting for the "long term" often choose to incorporate. This allows the contractor to bill on a corp to corp basis, which allows for the potential to eventually expand your one-person corporation and bring others on board.

There are some companies that will not work with incorporated consultants, but most will. Generally, you spend more time running your business of one, and dealing with the tracking of expenses that relate to your corporate profit and loss, but there are significant tax advantages to this arrangement.

If you like micro-managing your finances and paying less in taxes overall, incorporating may be a good option for you. Although the IRS does frown on one-person corporations, they are not auditing them at this time nearly as frequently as they are auditing 1099 independent contractors who are not incorporated (avoid this third type of contracting altogether).

There is an art to knowing when to contract. In general, you are contracting in order to cash in on a specific expertise. Contracting means that you are taking that expertise and utilizing it again and again for different clients. There is the danger that, over time, you will become too focused, which is why some choose salaried consulting even though contracting generally pays much better. As a general rule, salaried consultants have a much greater ability to transition their skills into new SAP modules and take the additional courses that the consulting firms will often pay for, since they are investing in your future.

One word of advice about salaried consulting: if you do go on salary, choose a full service consulting firm with a real career path and commitment to training. Avoid a "body shop" environment. If all a consulting firm is doing for you is billing you out and securing new projects, why bother? You can do that yourself and make significantly more money.

The best time to become a salaried consultant is when you are trying to fill in the gaps in your skills. For example, if you have SD experience in gap analysis and design but no configuration skills, you are not generally in a position to contract. You should choose a salaried consulting position with a company that commits to filling in that gap in your skills. If you have achieved a marketable sub-niche within a particular module, such as a CO-PA job listing, then you may well be a nice fit with the contract market. As a general rule, those who have general SAP skills but lack a specific skill focus will have a harder time contracting. But if you have sustained work in a particular module, such as FI-AR or SD with heavy pricing, especially if you have relevant industry experience in accounting or sales information systems respectively, then you might be ideal for contracting.

You do not need previous consulting experience to contract. While it is a major plus, you do not need salaried consulting experience with a Big Five consulting firm in order to contract. If your expertise is specific enough, you can move straight from an end-user permanent employee to contracting.

Project managers have a hard time finding contracts. This is not true across the board, but as a general rule companies want their project management expertise in house, or they rely on the chosen consulting firm to provide project management along with implementation methodology. Project managers are usually viewed as the authors or directors of an SAP production. As such, the credit, or pelt, goes to the consulting firm that supplies the project manager. Further, clients wants a company that can be held accountable, not an individual. In general, your contracting marketability depends on your hands-on skills.

Generally you cannot become a contractor and upgrade your professional level of responsibility at the same time. For example, it is hard to move from AM configurator on salary to AM team lead on contract. As a general rule, if you are seeking to move into leadership capacities or otherwise develop your resume in a significant way, you should look at salaried consulting before contracting. Contracting is more about money than resume enhancement, although the quality of projects you choose to contract on does have a major impact on the quality of your resume.

Contracting Lifestyles

The independent consultants we know offer largely positive reports on their chosen lifestyle, though they caution that working independent is not for everyone. The advantages include: freedom to choose the assignment that's right for you (as opposed to simply being assigned by your firm) superior hourly compensation, and no hassles with the management bureaucracy that can stifle those working with larger firms. At the same time, independent consultants caution those who are considering this option to think carefully about the potential instabilities of this arrangement.

Those who go independent understand that they could face unpaid bench time between assignments. In addition, they do not always enjoy the same kind of benefits packages that a permanent employment position provides. Those with family commitments tend to shy away from working on contract, primarily because permanent positions, though offering significantly lower compensation, come with a regular paycheck and full insurance benefits, important to the family and family budget planning.

As an independent contractor, you have three options: you can be hired on a W-2 basis, with taxes already deducted from your paycheck, or you can be hired on a 1099 basis, with no taxes deducted. With the 1099 model, you are responsible for making your own quarterly tax payments, but you have the advantage of numerous expenses and deductions. The third option is to form your own corporation and then bill companies on a corporation-to-corporation basis. Although this is the most complex of the three options, it seems to attract less attention from the IRS than the 1099 status when it comes to auditing. As more corporations abandon the 1099 format due to the potential tax exposure, incorporating yourself seems to be a better and better option, offering many similar advantages is terms of deductions but with less tax liability.

The consultants we have worked with generally caution against the 1099 status, due to the IRS' increased auditing of these arrangements. This status may also lead to the hassles of dealing with your own tax payments and expense deductions, (all of which could be put under the glare of the IRS when tax filing deadlines come around). Most companies are no longer willing to hire employees as 1099ers for the same reason, but be very cautious about accepting this type of arrangement. As one independent told us, "One mistake and they're all over you."

Contracting Pursuits

If you decide to work as an independent consultant, you can either approach companies directly or work through outside consulting firms and recruiting agencies. The vast majority of Fortune 500 SAP implementations are staffed by Big Five firms. These firms are first looking within their own rosters before considering independents; it can be difficult to get in on your own. If you opt to do the hard work of marketing yourself and approaching companies directly, you have the advantage of not having to share your hourly margin with anyone else. On the other hand, you are now in the role of handling your own negotiations, a situation some consultants are more comfortable with than others.

It is not always easy to know what you are worth and how to get it in such a volatile marketplace. If you do decide to approach companies on your own, you should be aware that many companies will now only hire you if you are incorporated or on someone's legitimate W-2 payroll, otherwise the tax liabilities are too great. One option is to do the marketing and negotiating yourself, but then to have an outside firm "pass" your paperwork and handle your payroll processing and tax payments. This agency would bill the company for you and take a small override for their services.

The other option is to pursue contracts through consulting firms and recruiting agencies. Using this arrangement, the outside agencies do your marketing and help you to secure your required rate. They present you to their clients, set up interviews for you, and set you up as an hourly employee. Once the contract is secured, the firm will hire you on a hourly basis and bill the company. The advantage to going with an outside firm is that you can rely on their connections and their marketing. This is especially useful if you are wrapped up in a major SAP assignment and have limited time to search for work yourself.

Because these firms typically collect an hourly override for every hour you work, the drawback to this kind of arrangement is that you lose a bit of your hourly draw. But some consultants we have worked with prefer this kind of arrangement, mainly due to the difficulties of approaching companies directly and getting a foot in the door.

If you do opt to take a contract through an outside firm, you may want to ask them what kind of margin they are making on your hourly rate to ensure that they are not taking advantage of you. Do not simply shrug and be satisfied that you got the rate you wanted because it will be important for you to know what the client is paying for your services.

Body Shopping – Bottom Feeding

We have seen many instances of greed in the world of SAP placement. One particularly odious (true) story: a Michigan client needed an HR specialist and this 'lead' made it through three levels of headhunters until such a specialist was found at a firm I was working with. We were offered $140 per hour and $95 per diem but a detailed expense report had to be rendered on a weekly basis.

After he had spent more than two months at the client site, our HR consultant was told by our headhunter that the client no longer desired his services. Bothered by this cancellation, we looked into the situation and learned that the end client was paying $220 per hour plus actual expenses. Upon further questioning, we found that the headhunter who had contacted us was making $20 an hour plus the difference between actual expenses and our $95 per diem. Two other headhunters higher up in the food chain were divvying up the remaining $60 per hour.

Worse than this, the end client had not wished for our consultant to leave. Instead, they were told by the headhunter at the top of the chain that our consultant had left voluntarily but that a replacement had already been identified. Though we never found any direct evidence, we are convinced that the lead headhunter had simply found a way to make more money and so engineered the consultant switch in mid-project.

If your financial situation allows you the freedom to consider the instabilities of being an independent, you may want to seriously look at this option. In a pure financial sense, it is probably the best way to take advantage of the SAP marketplace. Although you don't get the prestige that is associated with employment with major consulting firms, you do get exposure to a variety of companies and industries. To get the most out of this option, consultants advise you to know the SAP market and your value within it.

Of course, you must be willing to travel (unless you are in an SAP-rich locality), and willing to spend some time on the bench between contracts if necessary. And some independents have warned us that the feeding frenzy their resumes create can be exhausting. Many recruiters who call don't really understand the SAP marketplace or what you are looking for. They merely think they have a hot fish on the line and are trying to cash in on your expertise.

As long as you are prepared for these logistical challenges, going independent can provide freedom and financial satisfaction.

Cut to the Chase – How to Skip Body Shoppers and Market Yourself

There are so many ways in which contract SAP consultants can market their own services that we often wonder why any of them would sign up with a body shop service, only to pay anywhere from $10 to $30 *per hour* against their own billing. That adds up to $1600 to $4800 per month that is going to someone else. If all you do is split this difference with a direct client by taking the time to market yourself, you can increase your earnings significantly.

Get to Know the Project Managers

If you are working with a Big Five firm as a subcontractor, you will have potential access to other project managers in the firm. Introduce yourself. Offer a clean resume. Let it be known that once you have completed your current assignment, you would be pleased to discuss another. Ask for a reference from your current project manager. Spice that reference with another from a key client contact. You could ride the same Big Five firm wave as a subcontractor for years and years. One of this book's authors did just that.

To make yourself known amongst the other SAP consulting firms, send along a cover letter and resume, preferably via e-mail. The cover letter is your attention-getter and you should include mention of your expected hourly rate. Normally, this rate will be at least marginally less than the firm is billing out to clients and the potential margin for that firm will be attractive. Further, small and mid-sized SAP firms would be relieved to avoid the body shoppers, many of whom do not commit "their" resource for as long as is needed.

To find these firms, get onto the Web and search on "SAP Consulting" or refer to the back of this book for a registry of SAP consulting firms.

Build a Website

A single page website is easy enough to build and post. Include a click for a download of your resume. And invest the $50 or $100 it takes to use a service that will include your website in search engines, otherwise no one will ever see it.

Note: those SAP consultants we know who have websites are often ahead of others in the game of selling themselves. Recruiters appreciate the ease of reading a web-based resume. Further, your having a website will demonstrate your professionalism and your initiative and you will distinguish yourself from the hundreds of hired guns out on that SAP flatland.

One more note: do not include photos of your car or your dog or your girlfriend on your website. We have actually seen these included in a few websites intended to "sell" a consultant and can only wonder what these people were thinking.

Use the Newsgroups

Body shoppers dominate these newsgroups, but in many cases clients post directly and, with a little digging, you should unearth a variety of potential assignments.

The Pros and Cons of SAP Contracting: One Contractor's View

A seasoned FI contractor was kind enough to submit to our pointed questions about the ups and downs of SAP contracting. Her answers are honest and clearly stated and should be of great use to anyone considering SAP contracting. We purposely posed questions that would dig deeper than the financial perks and the answers are a mix of her replies and our own observations.

What do you see as the advantages to SAP contracting over other options? Are there any advantages besides the money?

1. The greatest advantages to contracting in any software is the **freedom and flexibility**. You can accept contracts at will and in any location. The advantage to contracting in SAP is there is plenty of work, so turning down unacceptable contracts is a real possibility as there is always another one available.

The advantage of contracting over working for a consulting firm is primarily freedom and autonomy.

Commonly, a consultant will leave a firm to work independently because their personal desires are not being respected in terms of job location, type of work, free time/bench time - sometimes it's money, but frankly the money is generally good in any event. Most people I know who left consulting firms to contract did so because they felt the consulting firm was not doing a good job meeting their needs or the client's needs. As a contractor you have complete control over who you work with and what you are committed to do.

As an example of how irritating the lack of control can be, the contracting firm I worked for before I went independent once brought me to an interview/sales call where the client explained I was being hired to configure and train their SD system. I had to explain that I was not qualified for this, I'm an experienced FI contractor with working knowledge of SD, but certainly not qualified to be an SD lead. The sales manager didn't know one module from another and had no real understanding of the depth of knowledge required to do the job. This kind of embarrassing and irritating situation is completely avoidable when you do your own sales. To be brutally honest, one of the advantages of contracting is not having to deal with managers who are completely clueless about the software!

2. A side-effect of the autonomy of contracting is I spend the vast majority of my time doing what I enjoy: working with the clients and the software. I spend **minimal time in meetings**, no time reporting to my management (as I have none) and minimal time on finding new work. Eliminating the consulting firm middle-man eliminated a lot of waste and frustration for me.

3. For people who want to work **non-standard hours** or schedules, contracting is the only type of job to have. I now work part-time and take off many weeks a year to spend time traveling or with my family. Very few firms are flexible enough to accommodate non-standard hours. As a contractor, if you can negotiate it, you can work it!

5. This might sound odd, but I believe contractors have more **continuity with clients** than salaried consultants. When a consultant is pulled off of a job, they rarely return, whereas companies will treat an independent as if they are an occasional employee, to be rehired when their services are needed. For me this is a positive side of contracting.

The money always seems great, but how does that weigh against the risks? What are the risks of contracting? Is the risk of bench time greater than as a salaried consultant, or less, because you have more control over your own marketing?

Contracting is riskier than consulting in terms of **cash flow**. If your contract ends prematurely or you find yourself without work for a while, it hurts. Most projects can only plan 1-2 months ahead (at most) for personnel requirements, but they need six- month commitments with potential extensions. If you don't have too many contacts, you could miss a window on some projects and have to wait for the next window to open. Further, there are seasons in which movement is swift and others in which no one is hiring anywhere.

The best time of the year to look for a new assignment is September 1 to October 30. The worst is between Thanksgiving and early January.

If you are willing to **travel**, this isn't much of a problem in the SAP market. If you are looking for local work, you may end up with some involuntary bench time. One candidate told us that she wanted to move to Tucson, Arizona and would not consider travel. Our advice to her was to prepare for six months of bench time between assignments.

Long-term projects are becoming more scarce as the Fortune 500 projects reach saturation point. The trend for the Millennium and beyond is shorter, ASAP-driven, project work of the 4 to 8 month stripe. Agility is more and more a requirement and bench time a greater threat for those who lack it.

One major risk with contracting is that of **getting stale** or falling behind on the current versions. Without a firm to train you, you have to take the initiative and make sure your contracts include some areas you don't know, or is on the latest software version.

Another problem with contracting is the **isolation** - you don't have any other consultants to lean on or ask for assistance. Project teams, especially those from certain big firms, tend to stick together and support each other. If you need additional training or wish to attend seminars or conferences, you do so on your own dime and the time you spend educating yourself is not billable.

A typical SAP contractor seldom has to deal with **bench time**, but when it happens, the repercussions are much worse for an independent than for a member of a consulting firm. The independent is losing both income and continuity when out of work, whereas a salaried consultant is just bored. On the other hand, we know many salaried consultants who have sat out long stretches waiting for their skills to be 'sold', but we know of few independents with that problem.

Does contracting make sense for a salaried consultant who would like to work their way into a management or partner-level position someday, or would it be a sort of detour away from the long-term goals?

We cannot imagine anyone thinking that contracting is a good career move towards anything other than further contracting. When you contract, you lose connections with your firm, your co-workers, and your old clients. Even if you were hired into a project as a project manager (which would be unusual, as most project managers are either in-house or from a large firm) it would not look as good on your resume as working the same position at a consulting firm.

People who gravitate towards contracting tend to be either truly independent folks who have no interest in moving into management or management-minded individuals who are temporarily setting aside their career goals in favor of short-term increases in pay.

Is the money in SAP contracting worth the risk?

Most consulting firms, SAP or not, keep a close eye on utilization rates, i.e. what percentage of a consultant's over-all time is billable. In essence, bottom line accounting for consultant firms takes into account the utilization rate required to break even on each consultant. Anything beyond that target rate will result in a profit. Some firms share back this profit in the form of bonuses.

Example:

John Vestsuit is an SD module leader. Between salary, benefits, material costs (laptop, overheads, etc.), and admin, he costs the firm $200,000 per year. If his billable rate is $150 per hour, he must perform 1,333 billable hours for the firm to break even. There are roughly 2,000 standard billable hours in a year (240 working days), so Mr. Vestsuit must have a utilization rate of roughly 65%.

Sixty-five percent utilization may not seem like much if the sailing is smooth, but what happens if there are three different assignments in the year and a month of bench time between each one? Add in ten to fifteen days per year for ongoing training. Kick in that week in February when John was under the weather. Add another 20 days for internal meetings, admin, and other. And John does get 15 days of vacation per year. So:

> 240 working days
> - 40 bench days
> - 15 training days
> - 5 sick days
> - 20 internal days
> - 15 vacation days
>
> 145 billable days ~ 1,450 hours @ 10 per day

Salaried consultants receive the same pay each month whatever the number of hours are billed for their services. Indies who go for the hourly gold learn that Merry Christmastime, when firms often close for two weeks, translates into a short paycheck. Ditto for any period in the year when project work is halted or while you are between gigs.

There are vast numbers of SAP consultants who prefer to remain independent rather than accept a $120,000 base salary with another $10,000 to $20,000 in bonuses. The reasoning is often based upon poor math skills on their part. All they can see is $125 an hour times 40 hours per week = $5,000. That comes to, oh, around $250,000 a year, give or take a few weeks on a Caribbean beach.

The real math must take into account:

1. Bench time while looking for an assignment
2. No 401K plan
3. No health benefits, no life insurance
4. Self Employment Tax
5. Training costs (and related expenses)
6. Costs for a laptop and whatever software you use

The annual cash value of elements 2 through 6 is $20K to $40K. Your actual billing time will usually be about 75% of the year, so you will gross about $195,000 (2080 hours * 75% = 1,560; $125 * 1560 = $195,000).

The lack of career path may or may not be a factor in this decision. Hired guns cannot work more than 365 days a year. That is the absolute ceiling unless you are twins. However, an employee can a) be promoted, b) receive stock options, c) become a partner and receive a share of profits, or d) transfer to another part of the firm and change career paths.

Is the risk worth the reward? There is no absolute fulcrum on which you can base your decision.

To illustrate, here is the point of view of our seasoned and articulate SAP contractor:

> "For me, as a single, mobile person, there are no cons about contracting. The usual cons that people think of are: no health benefits, no disability, no pension, no 401K and no job stability. First, I only spend about $1800 a year on medical benefits. Second, disability insurance costs me $1300 a year for a tax free benefit of $70,000 a year. Third, I set up my own paired pension plan (Money Purchase & Profit Sharing combined) under my corporation, to which I can contribute up to 25% of my salary tax deferred. Fourth, any matching contributions you might receive in a 401K plan would be no more than around $4000 a year.
>
> Lastly, there is no more job stability in corporations today, employees are now in more fear of being laid off than the contractors because they don't have the network of contacts which contractors tend to have. So, where companies will tell you that their benefits package adds up to 30% of salary or more, you can see that my reckoning is (1800 + 1300 + 4000) or about $7000 a year. Add to that the additional

social security and Medicare payroll taxes (about $4500 a year) and accounting costs (for me, about $800 a year), and the total cost of being incorporated is no more than $13,000 a year. Contractors with families will pay an extra few thousand for medical benefits. Now, at $100 per hour, you are making about $200,000 a year, compared to about $100,000 as an employee - its a mathematical no-brainer.

If you go contracting, incorporating is the way to go, mainly because of the expense write-offs which I will not detail, but also because of the 25% of salary which you can save pre-tax. Many people mistakenly think that an incorporated contractor is a '1099'. This is false, corporations do not issue other corporations 1099s, they only issue them to individuals who are not employees such as self-employed people. Self-employed is another way to go, only now you will get issued a 1099 at year's end. The advantage is that the total employer and employee social security taxes are about 12% versus 15.6% for incorporated.

The disadvantage is that expense write-offs must wait until year's end to show up on Schedule C of your personal return, whereas a corporation can reimburse you at any time during the year. Also, the maximum you can save pre-tax is 15% in a SEP. The third way to go is a 'W-2' contractor where you are now an employee of the consulting company that's paying you. You can still claim expenses on Schedule C, but hourly rates will be less as your employer charges you for the additional payroll taxes, insurance and who knows what else which they incur. The most you can now save pre-tax is $2000 a year in an IRA."

Lifestyle and finance. Career path and job identity. Opportunity and risk. Weigh all of these before making your decision.

Case Studies

No one in this market has a perfect ability to make the right career choices, and it goes without saying that hindsight is always 20/20. Nevertheless, we think a critical evaluation of these choices will be helpful to you as you weigh out your own options.

The good thing about the SAP market is that it is relatively forgiving. There is some margin for error, and almost always a chance to regroup if the wrong path is taken as long as the necessary change is identified and made quickly. You may be surprised how fast your skills can decline if you end up on the bench, or on the wrong type of project.

The following case studies are intended to be instructive but can be viewed as your self-test in regard to the lessons of this book. Read each case story and then stop for a moment to reflect on which decisions you would make before reading the conclusion.

Case Study One: ABAP/4 Contractor – Texas

We once worked with an ABAP/4 contractor who liked to stay local to Texas metros. Fortunately, Texas is one of those areas of the country where you can contract, and with some effort and a bit of luck, be able to stay local and not have to travel to make the contract rates. This individual was a pretty seasoned ABAP/4 programmer with a little more than three years of experience overall, all in R/3. He did not have any version 4.0 experience, but had plenty of experience in 3.1x. During his three years of ABAP/4 work, this individual had managed to cover the range of ABAP/4 responsibilities, including BDC, RFC, report generation, some custom development work, and even a bit of SAPscript. He had programmed in several of the major modules, including FI, SD, and MM. FI was his strongest suit.

On the "down side," this contractor did have some potential areas to improve. Although he had good communication skills and a decent functional understanding of SAP, he had never served in a ABAP team lead role. In truth, he was not sure about team lead work and whether he would like it. He did not want to get too far away from the technical work. However, we encouraged him to think of team leadership as a chance to balance hands-on work with technical lead work. The next step up from a team lead role might be a project management role (where in the Fortune 500 space you could lose your hands-on exposure), but these steps are clearly delineated. Just because you take one step up does not mean you are forced to keep traveling further up the corporate food chain. (In fact, as an ABAP/4 contractor, you probably do not want to advance much further than team lead. There aren't that many technical project management positions available to contractors).

The other possible area for improvement for this contractor was in the oft-mentioned area of "integration technologies." This programmer had never had any exposure to EDI, workflow, ALE, Internet/Java work, or SAP-BAPI development work. In addition, this programmer had never worked in the HR module, and anything SAP/HR-related was and is pretty hot at the moment.

In our discussions with this contractor, we encouraged him to think about the fact that as the market matures, and offshore ABAP groups have an impact on rate, that he may find himself one of many ABAP/4 programmers with solid experience programming in FI, SD, or MM. We felt that he could make some nifty additions to his skills in one of the three areas above: team lead, integration technologies, or ABAP-HR work. Any of these three would have been a helpful addition to his skills. Further, he would not be facing a major, ambitious change like switching to functional consulting nor would he have to switch to a permanent, salaried position to make these changes. This ABAP programmer was one of those fortunate folks who was in a pretty good position to really enhance his skills while remaining a contractor.

Furthermore, we encouraged this contractor to think less in terms of the ABAP-HR move than the team lead or integration technologies options. It is pretty clear that at some point the supply of ABAP-HR contractors will catch up with demand, whereas the first two options are more "visionary," and would solidify a long-term career marketability. The team lead experience would leave open a wide range of challenging leadership positions and push his experience closer to business-minded programming, thinking in terms of team objectives and overall project scope issues.

The integration technology exposure would be equally forward-thinking, as it would help him to become part of the "extended ERP" employment world that is coming up on the horizon. The only catch is that we had some concern that given this contractor's geographical restrictions, he would not be able to find one of these "skills enhancement" contracts by the time his current engagement ended. However, we felt that it was still a good idea to shoot for this type of position, lining up other general ABAP assignments as a fallback. We also encouraged this contractor to be more flexible on rate if he had the chance to move forward with his skills. A bit less money per hour on a contract is worth more money than there would be by taking a salaried position to retool your skills.

As it turns out, this contractor was unable to find an "integration technologies" project that met his geographical and time restrictions. This happens sometimes, especially when you're trying to break into something new on an hourly basis. He was, however, able to come up with two assignments: both were long term projects (one year plus), and both had fairly attractive rates.

Option 1: an ABAP-FI team member role at $130 an hour.
Option 2: an ABAP team lead role for $120 an hour.

Both were version 4.0 projects, an important consideration. In both cases, the projects were commutable so geography was not an issue.

[Reader: close this book and reflect for one minute before continuing on. What would you have done? Ten dollars an hour = about $400 a week before taxes. But $120 an hour is already $4800 a week before taxes.]

The Decision

This contractor chose the $130 an hour project, opting for the additional $10 an hour in compensation.

Our Assessment

While we appreciated that an additional $10 an hour was at stake here, we felt that this was a relatively small amount when balanced against an opportunity to take on a team lead role. Of course, this contractor might have found that the team lead role was not the right one for him. As it stands, he will never know.

In terms of building his long term professional net worth, as well as making himself more "recession-proof" in this increasingly crowded market, we felt that he had passed up a golden opportunity. In the immediate term, a cost of 7.5% less income might have led to mid-term rates of much more. Further, the team lead role would have opened up more "career advancement" options in a permanent consulting setting.

Obviously, this contractor made the conservative, and financially driven decision to capitalize on his current core skills. The longer rates hold out for experienced "general function" ABAPers like him, the better his decision will look. And obviously, he will have the opportunity to reassess his rate options in a year's time. One thing that has to be said for this contractor: he was able to lock in a slightly-above-market ABAP rate for a significant period of time. We wish him well on this project and we both look forward to taking up this debate in a year, to find out "who was right" and why. For now, we agree to disagree.

Feedback

The preceding case study was on our website and we did receive several vigorous letters from ABAP developers in response. The gist of these letters was: "Why is everyone always pushing ABAP programmers to become team leaders? Some people just aren't natural team leaders and don't want to be. Let us do what we are best at, developing SAP functionality for our clients. We don't want to go the project management route. If we did, we wouldn't be contracting."

Fair enough. The vertical path, especially since the mid-80s, is not for everyone. However, there are some important considerations to keep in mind. We believe that there are three main skill paths for technical SAP folks. One path is to remain strictly as a programmer, hands-on, doing the programming (or Basis work) that you do best. This option can be pursued either as a contractor or permanent employee. No one is obligated to become a team lead in order to further a career. However, keep in mind that just because you become a hands-on team lead does not mean that you are now on a rigid career path which ends up in hands-off project management. Whether or not team lead positions appeal to you, it is important to recognize that you can become a team lead without ever moving any higher. It can be a nice way to have a hands-on career, along with some additional leadership skills that not only enhance your market value, but also give you more impact and control over your portion of the SAP projects you are on.

The team lead option is the second of three main career options for SAP technical folks. The third option is to eventually move into a project management role, after spending some time as a team lead. But you are not required to move further away from the technology if you are not so inclined. Hands-on team leaders with no desire to advance further are best served by the contract market, where the pressures from management to move up the food chain are less prevalent. Those team leaders who want to eventually become project managers would be better served by eventually taking a position as a permanent employee. No, team leadership is not for everyone, but it does not imply an inevitable climb into upper management either. It is simply one good direction to take if you are looking to make your SAP skills "recession-proof."

One final point to consider: an SAP project is different from the traditional IT project. Unlike the classic "back room" coding project, SAP is clearly business-driven. For this reason, there is much less tolerance in the SAP market for those technical folks who would like to sit in front of a computer all day and not concern themselves with the challenge of working with other team members. The successful SAP technical person does not need to be a manager or even a team leader, but we do believe that strong communication skills and a solid business understanding are necessary for virtually all who succeed in this field.

There is room for a few genius developers (code crunchers in leathers and t-shirts), who are lacking in social graces, but not as many as you would think, and certainly less than on the low-profile IT project of old. The SAP project site is typically a culturally diverse environment that does demand a more sophisticated, business-oriented approach.

Case Study Two: FI/AR Northeast

An FI functional specialist living in the NY/NJ area is our next case study subject. She graduated from college in the early '90s, and has been with the same company since then. She has acquired a decent amount of accounting-related skills over the years, as well as some business process redesign work that took place before SAP came along.

When her company decided to implement SAP, she was drafted from the accounting department to work with the outside consultants throughout the implementation process. Unlike some end-user employees, she was actually allowed to perform all the implementation tasks right alongside the consultants, including heavy configuration work. Better yet, she was able to obtain experience throughout the implementation cycle, from the early gap analysis and process design phase, all the way through configuration and testing and into end-user training.

This consultant was making about $60K at the point she decided to make a change. We saw her as making a bit less than the norm for end-users and she was aware that she could potentially make more as a consultant. At the time she contacted us to discuss her career and her marketability, the implementation had gone "live" in her area. She was at a point where her duties were balanced between maintenance mode cleanup, end-user training, and a return to her accounting functions. It seemed like a good time to assess her options and see if a career in SAP might be the right one for her.

The prospect of additional compensation certainly interested her quite a bit, but the challenge of consulting and future professional growth was her main motivation for looking around. At the time she contacted us, she had a year and a half of full-time involvement in SAP, including configuration. However, she was on a large implementation site, so her configuration skills were limited to FI-AR (accounts receivable). She wanted to know what her marketability might be. Travel did not pose a problem.

Our initial feedback: although she had never been a consultant, she did have strong communication skills and had done quite a bit of 'internal consulting' on her project. We felt certain that she had the demeanor to succeed as a consultant. Since she was open to travel, we advised her to seriously consider consulting, and to take advantage of the chance to work on multiple implementations and really become an expert in her field. Her industry experience of about seven years was enough to look solid on paper, and all of her work experience was finance-related and fit in well with her SAP FI skills. It made sense for her to think about continuing to flesh out her functional FI skills, perhaps adding some CO exposure as well.

We discussed the option of contracting, but she didn't feel confident enough in her SAP skills and we agreed that the best next step would be to work with a firm that could expand her skills. The good news was that she did have the configuration skills that are necessary for functional SAP success, but the bad news was that since she was very focused in FI-AR, she wouldn't be appealing as an independent without a broader base of knowledge. We also felt that smaller consulting firms would be an unlikely option, as the smaller consulting firms generally need a higher degree of implementation experience. She certainly wasn't ready to be the only FI person on a project site yet

.

Larger firms, however, posed problems as well. In a larger consulting firm, she might have ended up on a large project just working on the piece of FI that she already knew. We did not believe that FI-AR was marketable enough to justify such a focus. We were also concerned that a larger firm wouldn't be as likely to get her exposure to the growing SAP mid-market. Getting ASAP certified was one of her main goals, and this wasn't as likely to happen with a larger firm.

The other problem was that several of the major consulting firms were engaged on her firm's project and she couldn't be hired by them, due to the "non-compete/no-hire" agreements that were in place. In truth, she wasn't certain that she wanted to join a large consulting firm. She liked the "prestige factor" of the larger firm, but the prospect of a smaller consulting firm with an entrepreneurial environment was very intriguing to her. Clearly, her skills and background posed some dilemmas, but we were certain that somewhere out there was the right opportunity and we were all determined to find it.

Hampered by this candidate's SAP skills limitations, the search went slowly. Instead of the "feeding frenzy" that sometimes can result when you begin to look at outside options, there were evenings when her phone did not ring at all. However, over a period of about six weeks, several interesting options presented themselves. She interviewed well, and in the final analysis two offers were put on the table, offers which could not have been more different.

Offer number one was from a large consulting firm with a strong technical focus. The firm had a few larger projects in mind for this consultant. Although our candidate liked the people she interviewed with, she wasn't sure who she would be working with closely. In other words, there were pleasant associations but no sense of a future "mentor." The firm had told her that she would receive additional training as well. The offer was $80K, a decent increase, along with an SAP skills bonus, to bring the total package into the $90K range. It seemed like a good increase, a fair one, but our consultant wasn't blown away.

Offer number two was from a smaller SAP consulting firm, with less than 50 consultants. Although the firm was small, its partnerships with SAP were in place and so access to further training and certification were available to our candidate. The partners running the firm were very accessible throughout the interview process, and our applicant felt that she would be able to consult with them on a frequent basis to reassess her career. She had the sense that they were willing to make an investment in her career and she liked the accessibility between her and the top players in the firm. Unlike other smaller firms, this firm was actually looking for some junior members to go along with its senior team. Better yet, they even had a project in mind for her, where she would serve as a junior FI consultant, working in FI-AR but also getting exposure to other areas.

It was clear that the client would know in advance that she was junior, but everyone was pleased because the rate was going to be discounted accordingly. The financial package seemed both superior and more risky than the larger firm's offer. The base was lower, in fact it was $60K, the same as what she was already making. However, our candidate would have a more sizable billing bonus, based on her projected net earnings. In a worst case scenario, she might make $90K or so; in a best case scenario, her income might reach the $110K range. The optimistic assumption was that her billing rate would go up over the course of the year and that she would be productive on projects.

In truth, this job-seeker was torn between the two options. The larger firm had some very important positives. One was the name recognition, and her confidence that its business extended far beyond SAP. It was clear that the chances to cross-train outside of SAP were better in this larger firm, as the smaller firm was entirely SAP focused. She also knew that a smaller firm, in addition to less name recognition, could be less stable. It is more likely to fold or merge with another firm. The travel seemed to be a wash. Both firms would have her on the road a fair amount. The money looked better at the smaller firm, but the billing bonus arrangement was a bit new to our candidate and she was uncomfortable with the notion of starting with the same base salary as she already had. The total package *looked* better, but it seemed like less somehow.

Further, our candidate had always worked in a large company. She was familiar with the sense of security that you can feel in the best of circumstances with a larger firm. The smaller consulting firm had a more entrepreneurial attitude. There was more room for her input, that much was clear, but there was also more expectation that she be self-directed and more involved in shaping her career path. That was an exciting challenge, but also daunting. It involved leaving familiar environments. The smaller firm was also hard to research. It was hard to find people who had heard of it and could vouch for it. In terms of opportunity for advancement, both firms seemed to have some opportunities. It seemed to her that equity positions were out of the question in either scenario. The larger firm was publicly held and the smaller firm had pretty clear equity positions already established.

The Decision

Although our candidate was leaning towards the smaller firm, she could not shake her fears about its relative "smallness". These fears were allayed through her frequent talks with the partners of the firm as they made it clear to her that they were committed to her future and had a good plan for her and a good collaborative spirit. In the end, she held her breath, and "took the plunge" with the smaller firm.

Our Assessment

We agreed with this decision, although we did understand her trepidation. It could not be denied: she had taken the "riskier" option, and it was natural for her to have some ongoing concerns. We did not think in this candidate's case that money was the crucial factor. Expanding her skills beyond FI-AR was the top priority, as that niche is too narrow. At the same time, we do favor arrangements that put more of the billing rate into the consultant's pockets. No doubt all of her concerns about the smaller firm's more precarious place in the market were valid. In our assessment, what tipped the scales was not the size of the firm but the ongoing commitment and communication made by the partners of that firm to the applicant. They helped her to see which project she would be on, and talked her through how that would benefit her.

By contrast, recruiters at the larger firm failed to demonstrate a career path, nor did they stay in touch with the candidate during the decision-making process. She did not get the sense from the larger firm that anyone powerful there was taking "ownership" of her well-being.

The fact that the smaller firm took the time to identify with her exactly how she would be able to expand beyond her FI-AR skills was also crucial. It is not enough that they pursued her. Plenty of firms will offer pursuit, as you readers out there know by now, but they genuinely understood her career dilemma and, in a problem-solving spirit, identified the right next step for her.

The large firm, in our opinion, rested too much on its reputation. And we all know that no matter what the size of the firm, you can wonder about the stability of your job. In fact, the larger firm can sometimes give you the impression that you are just a dot on a skills grid, and that sensation does not lend itself to a sense of well-being. We felt that the worst case scenario wasn't all that bad. If things didn't work out at the smaller firm, she could very likely revisit the opportunity with the larger one. We talked in detail with her about how to leave things on good terms with the larger firm so that she would have the option of coming back in the future.

In the final analysis, we felt that the larger firm would be able to revisit her situation in six months or a year's time. The opportunity at the smaller firm was more time-sensitive (who knew if they would have the same junior level opportunity on an FI project six months from now?).

Case Study Three: HR and Market Rate

The two preceding cases pivoted upon career advancement rather than money. We are aware that in some cases, capitalizing on market rate is the essence of the job search.

Let's take a look at an HR consultant who had a slightly more complicated job decision recently that brought the issue of "market rate" to the forefront. This HR consultant had graduated from college with a degree in marketing in the mid-'90s. He had four years of experience in industry. During this time, he had worked in several capacities involving marketing and human resource-related responsibilities for two different companies. At the second company, he was drafted onto the SAP HR implementation team. Up until this point, this future SAP professional had no real software or IT-related experience. He had not chosen a career in human resources; in fact, he took the position simply because he was very interested in working for this particular company and building a career from the inside. This was the definitive "lucky SAP break." This person did not anticipate a career in SAP; SAP found him.

When we first spoke with him, he had just over a year of experience in SAP, and been through the HR implementation process. He was lucky enough to have spent a good deal of time configuring gross and net payroll.

Although he had not intended to move into an SAP career, frequent calls from recruiters and discussions with outside consultants soon convinced him that SAP could be an exciting career choice. At the very least, he could now sense that his skills had market value. He did not have any prior consulting experience, but he was drawn to the consulting field and thought SAP might be the way in.

There were lingering questions about the travel involved. Some travel sounded nice, but "year in, year out, Monday through Friday" work seemed a bit much. His salary was close to $50K, including a modest bonus. He was comfortable with his salary based on his total work experience but was not at all opposed to an increase. (Who would be?) Further, he was based in the NY/NJ area, where the cost of living is relatively high.

His interview process was like a whirlwind as his candidacy resulted in more offers than he'd anticipated. The highest paying offer was for a total package of $120K (from a firm that interviewed him on the phone for no longer than a half hour before faxing an offer letter to him). Eventually, he had to stop taking offers and concentrate on the six or seven that he had on the table.

One firm in particular was intriguing. It promised him regional travel, and the firm even brought him onto a client site close to where he lived so that he could meet the team he would be working with on his first assignment. The knowledge that at his first project was going to be a local one was very appealing to him. Still, he knew that the promise of regional travel can be difficult to keep. To answer his concern, the firm took the trouble to meet with him several times to give him a thorough understanding of how they worked and what they had to offer. This firm came in with an offer of $75K plus 20% in bonuses. It was not the highest offer he had received. In fact, it was one of the lower ones, but it seemed like a comfortable increase and a great total package compared with his current salary.

Generally, we see a real benefit to salaried consulting, especially earlier in a career, where broad skills exposure can be a real benefit of full time employment, but in this case, we thought that contracting might deserve a closer look. We encouraged this individual to think about independent contracting as well before he made his final decision. This was due to his SAP niche in HR. As mentioned in our chapter on rates, SAP HR is the one area in the current SAP market where you can still "write your own ticket" with just one year of implementation experience and no consulting experience. In the United States, the hottest HR area is gross and net payroll configuration (North American payroll), and this man's single year of experience in this area was potential gold.

Given this window of opportunity, we felt that this candidate should look at one contract offer, to see what type of hourly rate he could achieve as a contractor. Even though we knew that he was not going to make a career in HR, we felt that the financial returns were so promising that he should seriously consider contracting, if only for a limited time. At his age, it would be a terrific time to sock away a large amount of money and provide a future funding source for purchasing a home, retirement, etc. We were confident that $125 an hour was an achievable rate. However, this candidate was skeptical about going off "on his own" and he just hadn't ever thought of himself as a "hired gun." Our reply was that the employment route would still be open to him after he completed a contract job or two and that, in essence, he could have the best of both worlds.

The Decision

This individual just didn't feel comfortable with contracting, and went with the consulting firm that offered him a regionalized travel opportunity.

Our Assessment

It is hard to question this particular decision. As we have said many times, every person has different priorities and needs. However, we feel that the SAP HR area offers some unique cash-rich opportunities that have to be taken seriously. Sometimes it really is best to take advantage of your hourly rate and not give up as much of it as you do for salaried consulting. Although this person did not want a career in HR, we still felt that contracting was a consideration that should have been taken a bit more seriously, at least until one contracting offer was on the table. It made sense to us to take the process at least that far. Given the active SAP market in the northeast region, this candidate would not have had to travel as much as contractors in other areas of the country. Although such advice flies in the face of our usual SAP advice, which is to stick with your "core competencies" and build on them, we feel that SAP HR presents the kind of opportunity that you truly have to "get while it's hot," even if you do not intend to pursue a career in HR information systems. We may be wrong, but we think this person will probably be contracting within the year.

Case Study Four: We Shop to Stop the Job Hop

The preceding case studies have concerned individuals with relatively light SAP experience, a year and a half or less. Now we will turn our attention to a more senior consultant, a woman who was facing a turning point in her SAP career.

Based out of the Midwest, our candidate had several years of significant SAP experience. Her initial strengths were in SD configuration. She got her start in SAP on an end-user site, where she was drafted for the "distribution" side of SD, based on her extensive knowledge of her company's pricing schemes and vendor/supplier/customer relationships. She did not have a sales background, but she did have significant experience managing key vendor accounts and she understood the critical importance of service management to her company's objectives. On the SD side of the project, she obtained significant configuration experience in many areas of SD, including order fulfillment and pricing.

Obviously, she was in the perfect position to be snapped up by a Big Five consulting firm, and two years before calling us, that is exactly what had happened to her. Extensive travel did not pose a problem for her; in fact, she was one of those consultants who really enjoyed the travel and could honestly say that the lifestyle of the consultant suited her. When she got her first Big Five offer, it didn't blow her away. She was making a salary in the high $60s at her end-user employer, including all bonuses, and the Big Five made her offers in the $80s plus bonuses.

It was a nice bump, but the main reason for leaving her company was to continue in SAP. She enjoyed the challenges posed by new implementations. Once her portion of that first SAP project was complete, she found that her company was interested in capitalizing on some of the gains of the implementation and were officially in a "low investment maintenance mode" that left her with few challenges. The SAP market has changed significantly in the last two years, but the difficulties end-users have in retaining their employees remains a constant for these very reasons.

Our SD consultant spent more than a year at a Big Five firm, but she received a number of calls from recruiters throughout the year (surprise, surprise) and as the year went on she started listening more closely to the opportunities. She was not dissatisfied with her Big Five firm, but the opportunity to make more money in a smaller, entrepreneurial environment was very appealing. Eventually, she left for a smaller firm that took her breath away with a $120K base salary and a 25% bonus, much of it guaranteed.

When she left, the Big Five firm tried in vain to keep her by offering her a $10K pay raise, but it was a case of too little, too late. Had they made a pro-active attempt to recognize her increased marketability, she might have stayed on, but the extra money offered by the smaller firm really was tempting. In retrospect, this was one of those somewhat spontaneous SAP job changes that seldom look sensible from a distance. At some point, to keep a bit more continuity in your resume, you want to make more strategic decisions, and our consultant recognizes that now, but back then she just had an impulse to follow the money. Further, her new firm looked good and her suitors said all the right things. It was a bit like a whirlwind romance without a lot of close scrutiny.

However, after a year at this new firm, the SD consultant contacted us. She was finding life at this firm was not exactly as she had hoped. There seemed to be a real scramble for new work. There was a lot of "body shopping" on other people's projects, and the sense of community that seemed so appealing at first had deteriorated into that claustrophobia of working too closely with flawed leadership. The SAP consulting marketplace had become pretty crowded and this firm seemed to lack direction. There was little focus in terms of industry or geography and there were rumors that the firm was about to be bought by a larger firm in a merger. Some of our candidate's friends at the firm were on the bench or traveling much farther than had been promised (the travel wasn't an issue to her, but broken promises were).

All in all, our candidate had begun to regret her decision to join that firm without having first looked at other options. She was also concerned about the perception of too much job-hopping on her resume and she wanted to find some place to settle into for a decent duration.

We shared her concern about the job-hopping perception, but the SAP marketplace creates a strange career situation. Given the supply shortfall, SAP consultants move more often than do other consultants and enlightened hiring managers tend to be forgiving of multiple positions in a short time frame. But the more skills you acquire and the higher up on the food chain you get, the more likely you will find yourself in a job search for a high-level position you really want. In such instances, you may find yourself dealing with a hiring manager who is still thinking "old school" and wonders if you lack direction. This type of person will grill you during the interview and might perceive you as a rate mercenary or a hired gun. At best, the perception of too-frequent job-hopping is a hurdle to overcome; at the worst, it limits your future opportunities. So our consultant wanted to make the "right move" this time and settle in for a while.

In terms of her skills, she had continued to focus on SD and now had three years of experience. SD-pricing configuration was a major expertise for her. She was well aware that she had enough skills to contract in SD pricing if she chose. All the same, this was not a niche that she really enjoyed. The potential of contracting money sounded nice, but the challenge of new skill areas and the perks of additional training attracted her to permanent consulting positions. During the previous six months, her current firm had pulled her into more pre-sales meetings, and while she enjoyed some of those challenges, she did not feel she was being compensated for her role as a revenue-producer signing up new clients. She also was not pleased about having become the firm's in-house "SD-pricing expert."

In terms of her long-term career goals, she had no problem thinking five years ahead. She was not as concerned with preparing herself to "get off the road" as some consultants are. Consequently, climbing the consultant ladder (project manager, then regional practice director) and eventually re-entering industry at a higher level (and higher salary) were not central goals for her. Although she fit our definition of the solid contractor, with her mastery of SD-pricing (a very marketable niche) she was more interested in continuing to expand her skills. She wanted to add MM experience to her SD skills, so that she would have more experience in areas pertaining to the logistics of materials management, distribution, and transportation, the backbone of the supply chain. She felt that this skills expansion would position her well for the "front office" work that SAP plans on obtaining in the coming years. Perhaps training in SAP's supply chain software could be added at a later point when the product was operational.

Beyond skills expansion, our candidate wanted to work with a firm that managed its own projects and did very little body-shopping. She liked the entrepreneurial environment of a smaller firm but it was important to her to get to know the leadership better before she was hired and thus have more confidence going in. She was satisfied with her current compensation and had no particular interest in advancement into project management; she wanted to maintain a hands-on role in SAP.

As the interviews loomed, our candidate established the areas that were important to emphasize (skills expansion in a company with a strategic vision and strong leadership), and which ones she would bend on (compensation and travel). In short, she had a vision of what she wanted and money was no longer the primary concern.

This consultant looked at a range of consulting firms. Some balked at her salary and many were not evolved enough to offer her the skills enhancement and project ownership she was looking for. Altogether, four offers were tendered, none from the Big Five.

Two of the offers were from "no frills body shops," and two of the offers were from career-oriented consulting firms. One of the no-frills firms offered her a $140K base with quarterly $5K bonuses. Another offered her a base salary of only $70K, but more than 55% of the total bill rate, for a total package of close to $220K if she was billable at least 80% of the time. One of the career-oriented firms offered her a lateral in compensation, but the promise of reduced travel, 50% or less. However, they had a SD-pricing project in mind for her right away and planned on addressing her training issues a bit further down the line. Another "career-oriented firm" had made a commitment to immediate training, along with a $5K increase in base salary and a $10K sign-on bonus.

The Decision

Although our candidate was tempted by the promise of the $220K total package offer, she also reasoned that this type of firm offered essentially a contractor's role at a slightly reduced rate, with less flexibility in choice of projects. She had already decided against becoming a contractor, so the first step in the decision-making process was to narrow the choice to the two "career oriented" firms. Although the promise of reduced travel had some appeal, she was concerned about the "immediate SD-project need" that this consulting firm was promoting for her. This type of "immediate need" is one of the yellow warning lights that reveal that a consulting firm may not be as far removed from a "body shop" as it might like to think. Even the most successful firms have to go through an evolution to get to the point of full control of projects and hiring for talent as well as immediate staffing needs. The promise of reduced travel had definite appeal, and might have been worth a lateral to another consultant, but this consultant had a bigger concern: expanding her skill set to stay one step ahead of other consultants. She was willing to endure some of the inconveniences of travel for this benefit of additional training.

In the end, she took the firm that offered her a modest $5K salary increase but seemed the most committed to developing her skills as a consultant.

Critical decision points were a) the company atmosphere was suitable and b) her training was included. She was immediately going to attend an MM certification course and an Inventory Management course was on the horizon. Further, this option supported her goal to blend MM skills with her already solid SD base.

Our Assessment

This consultant followed a very careful and thoughtful search process and it was hard to argue with her results. She knew exactly what she wanted and what she was willing to give up and this made the negotiations go very smoothly. We thought her desire to stay hands-on and to expand into MM, positioning herself for future SAP/supply chain opportunities, was a sound one. And since she was not currently managing projects, she really was not in a position to look at "Practice Director" roles that some very seasoned SAP consultants aspire to.

Following our approach that it is wise to look at the range of options, we thought she should have also considered an SD-pricing contract to take a harder look at the money there. SD-pricing is a good contract niche, but the fact that this candidate did not enjoy that work was a real warning sign.

We agreed with her that the "no frills" firms made little sense based on her rejection of the contracting model. And her commitment to building her skills, even if it meant putting up with bad airline food, seemed to reflect a good understanding of the tradeoffs of consulting. In the end, we agreed with her decision.

If this consultant had a greater fascination with becoming a senior SD-pricing specialist, it would have been a tougher fork in the road for her and a more difficult assessment for us. But all things considered, we think she made a good move.

Case Study Five: Taking You Far By Keeping You Nearby

We have already made the point many times: if you're not prepared to "hit the road" at some point in your SAP career, your professional prospects may be adversely affected. On the other hand, there are a number of successful SAP professionals who have managed to progress very well in their careers without ever leaving the comfort of their home town. It goes without saying that for some people, family considerations are more important than the career benefits of the consulting lifestyle. At the same time, those who are committed to low travel situations also want to enhance their professional prospects as much as they can without violating their primary commitments. Let's take a look at how such a search can play out, and in the process some of the key themes of this type of job search should emerge.

We were contacted by an HR functional specialist who could have made a great deal of money as a consultant. He was based on the West Coast and had a year and a half of HR implementation experience, including version 4.0 payroll experience, where the current rates are hovering not too far below the salaries of professional athletes. In addition, he had an MBA, and several additional years of HRIS experience implementing payroll systems. He also had some C and C++ programming experience, and was probably about 65% functional/35% technical.

This HR specialist felt that, at $60K plus $5K in bonuses, he was worth more in the open market. However, he did not want to travel. He also did not want to contract (for the purposes of this case study, let's ignore the contract option as this individual did, and focus on the main issue of low vs. high travel. Obviously, in some areas of the country, it is possible to contract locally without becoming a road warrior).

Fortunately for this HR specialist, he was not very concerned about whether or not he was being paid market rate. He was definitely committed to leveraging his skills to enhance his long term net worth, but he wanted to find a better way of doing that for himself than consulting. He was not willing to relocate (a very important consideration for those who don't want to travel, obviously), but he was fortunate in that there were about 8 to 10 ongoing SAP implementation within an hour's drive of his house. One thing was for sure: it was time to move on from his current employer, not because of compensation, but because of lack of challenge. The company was officially in "maintenance mode" and it was unclear just when there would be additional SAP work. Having been exposed to SAP, this HR specialist found himself very much energized by working on the project and definitely wanted to continue in an SAP career. He was not willing to wait until the powers-that-be at his company decided when they were going to move forward with new SAP functionality.

(Notice anything interesting here? A candidate ready to move, not because of compensation, but because of a stagnant work situation. We have long noted that this is what causes turnover in the SAP world far more than the lure of riches.)

As we reviewed this man's options in the market, we briefly considered the option of working for an SAP third party developer. There are a growing number of these third party firms, and they can be exciting places, often brimming with the possibility of equity/IPO, but also with a number of "red flags" related to mergers, buyouts, and associated market volatility. This was not the right option for this HR specialist, although if he had been interested in building on his programming skills he might have considered these 'third party' development environments a little more seriously.

So with these "third parties" pushed to "backup" status, we were left with a handful of local implementations. This is the scary aspect of the low travel search: would he be able to find a suitable position locally, or would he face relocation or the unsavory option (to him) of life on the SAP road? We both felt that it was important to keep a selective mindset and search for the best possible situation without worrying as much about worst-case scenarios. This meant applying additional criteria to the search process, even with only a handful of options to consider.

Several "differentiators" for evaluating prospective employers emerged: 1) the company had to be in the early phases of an SAP HR implementation and 2) this company had to have a convincing, long term commitment to continually upgrading and enhancing the SAP functionality. This applicant did not want to find himself back on the market every year of so when his new company's SAP implementation was over.

The frequent moves this man had already made had been stressful and would eventually chop up his resume and give almost the impression he was a contractor or SAP mercenary, not the goal he had in mind. This next implementation needed to be with a company that had "big dreams", perhaps including commitments to implementing SAP's employee self-service solution using the Internet. Our candidate was open to eventually looking at additional functions beyond HR, perhaps even to work with SAP's upcoming Sales Force Automation product, or perhaps in an SAP Business Warehouse initiative. A company with big, long-term plans for SAP and a major corporate commitment was important.

The third key screening criterion was that the company had to have an aggressive stock option plan for its employees. This HR specialist felt, and we strongly agree, that the best end-user opportunities include the perk of stock options. Stock options are a key component to long term net worth and help provide a hedge against the generally modest salary ranges paid by these end-user firms.

Of course, there were additional criteria that could have been considered, such as the size of the company, or the industry focus, or perhaps the company's reputation in terms of salary, but since the original pool of prospects was only about seven companies, it did not make sense to narrow the search too quickly. It was vital to keep an open mind and see which companies had genuine interest. As it turns out, there were only four companies of the seven that met all three major criteria above. One of the four never responded to his resume, and the second made a decision during the interview process to seek all of their functional resources through implementation partners, so the search quickly narrowed to two companies, both of which actively interviewed our HR specialist.

About four weeks later, he had two offers in hand. One was an $80K offer with a medium size company. There were no stock options, but there was a modest $10K bonus plan. Unfortunately for this consultant, there was a bit of international travel expected, possibly more than a bit.

The other offer was from a larger implementation that did have an aggressive stock option plan, as well as plans to implement a major SAP HR employee self-service initiative. No promises were being made, but an SAP Business Warehouse initiative was also being considered. The salary was $65K, but there were stock options awarded at the time of hire, as well as the promise of additional equity for milestones achieved. This stock was more "blue chip" in nature, perhaps with less chance for radical appreciation but also with less chance for radical dives to the basement of the market.

The Decision

It probably comes as no surprise that our HR specialist took the last job offer. The perk of additional exciting projects, combined with stock options and *low travel*, met all of his SAP search criteria. He was a bit edgy about what a "close call" he had in his search. After all, the margin for error was very slim, but he was glad to have secured a position with one of the few end-users in his areas that truly met his goals. Of course, no project is beyond revision, but it seemed as if the major job search issues had been resolved. Our HR specialist breathed a sigh of relief for avoiding a much more difficult crossroads (high travel or possible relocation), and set into his new project with vigor.

Our Assessment

We agreed with this decision-making process, and felt that this individual was realistic in terms of salary and career vs family goals.

He realized there were trade-offs and resisted the temptation to try to "have it all" when, in fact, some decisive commitments were in order. The big test will come when the phone starts ringing and much more lucrative offers roll in, but we think that this applicant thought through the pros and cons carefully. He might be tempted by some of the job offers, but he seemed ready and able to let go of being the best paid HR consultant in the market.

Although the other offer was significantly more money, the perk of stock options, along with the more appealing technical plans of the other company, were the key considerations. We agreed. If this applicant wanted money, he should have chosen a different path. (Indeed, if he had opted for contract consulting, his income would have been significantly altered...for a given period of time.) Continued skills enhancement was deemed more important, especially when he may eventually be competing for positions with seasoned HR consultants. He might have been missing the fast lane, but this person didn't care. Most of us have second thoughts, and that can be a poison for accepting more modest positions. Lifestyle versus career/cash is not always an easy balance, and we will not be surprised if these issues come up again.

SAP = Suitcase and Passport

The travel requirements of an SAP consultant are legendary. Here, we offer insight from various experienced consultants.

From Scott Gilbert, an independent consultant with experience in ABAP, EDI, ALE, and much more.

I hear now you can purchase a life using frequent flyer miles! That is valuable information to know the next time someone tells a consultant working 60 hours a week to get a life. Answer: just hold on a quick minute – I gotta call Delta and check on that !!!!!

You will finally find a Chinese restaurant with edible food the day before you roll off the client site.

If you have HERTZ GOLD and jump right into your car, you will find your price is wrong and your frequent flier number will be missing. When you go to the counter to get it fixed, all the other people on the HERTZ shuttle bus without GOLD service will have gotten there before you and you will wait at HERTZ for no less than 30 minutes.

No matter how many Delta miles you have, first class will be full.

No matter how you time it you will miss the following events:

1) children's first words
2) children's first crawl
3) children's first steps
4) children's first day at school
5) all of your children's Halloween's.
6) children's first visit from the tooth fairy.
7) Any cool party given by a friend on a Friday night or Sunday night.
8) The superbowl (but the Delta pilot will be kind enough to tell you the wrong score while you fly back to loserville, USA)

At least once per client site the bank will deposit your ungodly sized check into someone else's account (once you get direct deposit that is). Until you get direct deposit worked out, at least once your check will get mailed to you the day after you head back to the client site (making it valueless for another week or two). The time you really need the money the bank will hold the check for about 40 days because it is out of state and very large!

No matter how many calls you make, the hotel room will either have miniature sized beds, smoke-filled curtains, or no room service. If it does have room service, it was closed five minutes before you finally got to the hotel.

The client site will always want and/or expect you to work 50 hours and bill for 40 (a 20% reduction in salary for the math- challenged).

No matter how long your contract length was stated to be by the search firm that found you the client site, the client will tell you it is no more than 60 days (even if they keep you there for a year).

If the contract length site was 180 days or longer, either your wife will leave you, your dog will die, or your car will be stolen at the airport.

No matter where your client site is, it will involve no less than two plane flights (at least one with propellers instead of jets) and a drive of no less than one hour coming or going to the airport. Double that estimate due to snow for at least 4 months out of the year.

You will be the first person in US Air history to have your carry- on luggage lost by the airline.

You will always dress wrong the first day due to incorrect information from the headhunter.

When you finally get home looking for a home cooked meal, your wife will want to go out.

Visas and SAP

In the boom years of 1993-1995, when North America had only a shallow base of experienced SAP consultants, the shores were quickly crowded with German, Australian, South African, and Dutch consultants with R/2 backgrounds and some R/3.

Indeed, companies like Origin (Dutch), Plaut (German), and Spearhead (South African) have been prominent in the SAP consulting landscape across North America. In addition to these firms, many North American SAP consulting groups imported hundreds of SAP-savvy foreigners whose immediate and constant billing helped absorb relocation costs and the not inconsiderable HR costs.

However, the foreign boom is over. SAP training is far more abundant now than it was in those years. Over fifty North American universities have SAP curriculum. Until late 1995, there was not a single book about SAP in English. Today, there are more than sixty.

Companies no longer look kindly on applicants requiring H-1 visa sponsorship. It is the company's burden to handle the legal and paperwork expenses, basically to establish that the applicant has a necessary professional skill that a U.S. citizen cannot provide. As for SAP, companies large and small are less and less inclined to hire and sponsor an H-1 visa applicant who is not already residing in the United States. Perhaps through a combination of stereotyping and companies getting burned by here-today-gone-tomorrow contractors, there is a growing reluctance to fly in and sponsor an H-1 applicant for an SAP contract.

If you are currently overseas, you will have a much better chance of finding work in the states as a permanent employee than as a contractor. In addition, you may do better at larger firms who have the budget, staffing, and systems to handle visa processing. If you are already located or working in the States, your may have better luck securing contract assignments. There are also small firms that "hold" H-1 visas from assignment to assignment, and some companies are willing to hire from these firms.

In general, however, your willingness to consider permanent positions helps your prospects for employment as an H-1 visa applicant considerably. In the case of contract assignments, the delays in starting date due to the paperwork process is often enough to eliminate H-1 candidates from serious consideration. In many cases, SAP positions involve consulting at client sites, and this requires an ability to communicate in English, not only adequately, but with sophistication. Some companies are very reluctant to look at H-1 applicants for this reason as well.

Although ethnic bias certainly excludes some people from some firms, the primary obstacles facing an H-1 are logistical and economic, with a gray area in between, which you could call the challenge of cross-cultural working environments. Quite understandably, companies are reluctant to make the investment of time and money into hiring and sponsoring an H-1 applicant in such an unpredictable market, where loyalties on both sides are often short-term in nature.

The best news for those of you seeking employment in SAP as an H-1 applicant is that, despite the challenges and obstacles, your chances are much better as an SAP applicant than with almost any other information technology related skill. As a general trend, the SAP hiring market is topping out a bit, and this is affecting everyone, not just H-1 candidates.

Companies want more experience and lower rates. They want an immediate return on their investment. They want to clean up messy implementations with qualified professionals. If you have the option of attaining permanent residency at your current company, or as part of a new job offer, you should consider it seriously. In such a rapidly changing market, any potential obstacles to employment should be eliminated.

From 1995 to 1997, the legal/processing costs of securing an H-1 rose from an average of $2,000 to close to $10,000. If raising processing fees is part of a U.S. government initiative to persuade companies to hire more U.S. citizens, the strategy is working. Due to the expenses involved, it is particularly difficult now for an H-1 applicant to obtain a contract position in the U.S.

For those SAP professionals who would like to work in the States on an H-1 visa, a willingness to consider permanent opportunities will help your chances considerably. If your heart is set on contracts, try to plan a visit to the States so that you can be easily available for interviews. This will defer some of the initial expenses and help companies see that you are committed.

What About Imported Consulting Skills?

Despite all the talk of what a small world this is, there are vast differences in business cultures that make it difficult for consultants to be effective when crossing borders. The notion of 'people skills' takes on new significance in the SAP consulting fields and a professional approach that works wonders in Lyons, France may not play so well in Peoria, Illinois.

During the mid-'90s gold rush, it was noted that many of the European consultants who came to North America possessed deep

SAP experience but were hampered by shallow consulting background. As the SAP market has moved into a more mature era, many such consultants have gone by the wayside; others have learned the skills needed to endure in the North American business climate.

Despite our organization charts, North Americans tend to work in a consensus-driven fashion, which can drive some foreign consultants to distraction. One SAP consultant once remarked that Americans "never follow the directions" and it is true that our most endearing (and frustrating) trait is our 'individuality'. Since an SAP endeavor drives people to work in uniform harmony, that individuality can prove to be an obstacle.

For those of you who are contemplating a move to the United States and hope to use your SAP skills as a leverage, our best advice is that you initiate a parallel education in North American consulting methods and practices.

Securing the Future

Nostalgia Isn't What It Used To Be

...nor is the career path of anyone in the world, whether in information technology or gardening. Downsizing, outsourcing, consulting, temping, and a rock and roll economy/technology have led us all to new configurations of our futures. For most of us, the best that we can hope for is a loyal tribe and enough firewood to carry us through five winters. And you, reading this book, are either already into a six-figure income or on the path toward one, so you cannot complain about job security because that sixth figure tends to be the price of not having any.

All the same, there are a number of steps you can take now to ensure a promising career down the road.

Many of these steps are simple and general, and could apply to virtually any career. In addition, there are specific concerns an SAP professional should be aware of.

To avoid gaps in your employment future, address the following general points:

1. Work at your current job as effectively as you can, even if you are seeking new employment. Do your very best not to burn professional bridges and continually pursue additional responsibilities to enhance your expertise. A good network, built on a good work reputation, is a subtle but extremely valuable hedge against periods of unemployment. Always provide adequate notice to ensure the best references possible.

2. Always take advantage of continuing education and training. Pursue certifications and additional degrees at every opportunity. Know what's hot in your industry and make sure you obtain all the formal and informal training you can, even if it costs you some overtime hours to take that evening class.

3. Keep one eye open to great opportunities in your field, whether or not you are formally looking for a new position. Even while you are thriving in your current position, be on the lookout for the early signs of your own dissatisfaction or company instability, and make proactive career moves and job changes whenever possible.

4. Continually assess your short-term career situation in terms of your longer-term objectives. Having a long-term plan or strategy is invaluable in helping you decide your next steps. Examples: If you someday wish to start your own firm, you might decide to pursue SAP contracts in order to raise capital. If you envision a Manager of Information Systems role, you will want to pursue project leadership positions and expand your IS scope beyond pure SAP functions.

5. Cultivate an entrepreneurial mindset. Even if you plan to stay at your company a long time, start thinking of yourself as ultimately self-employed. Consider setting up a home office. Use the latest in desktop technology to create your own business cards and stationery and consider occasional side consulting projects. Investigate the option of incorporating or setting up a partnership with a business associate. Do these things now, while they are fun side projects. They may not seem as fun if you wait to do them when you find yourself out of work. Keeping a few sources of income active helps you to feel in control and gives you some flexibility in times of need.

In addition, there are specific concerns that all SAP professionals will want to consider. We caution people from capitalizing on a hot SAP market without considering their long-term priorities and fundamental expertise. SAP is a vast program with many niches; you should cultivate a niche that fits in with your general background and plans for the future. For example, if you are traditionally a programmer with a C++, C, and Cobol background, you should spend a good amount of your SAP time in the ABAP/4 programming area (unless you have made a permanent decision to move on from coding). Those with an MBA and finance background should likewise focus on areas of SAP that relate most closely to their financial expertise, such as the FI/CO modules. If your background is in manufacturing, you might want to focus on the MM/PP area. If you are a technical type with a Master's in computer science and a systems administration background, the Basis area would be a logical focal point.

The key point is to think of how you would describe your time in SAP if/when the boom is over. Wouldn't it be better to be able to say 'I have an MBA and a heavy accounting background. For the last three years I have been specializing in financial applications for corporate client/server settings' than to say 'I got into SAP because it was a hot area, ended up in manufacturing with a fair amount of coding and now I'm looking to get back into finance.'

Be mindful of your industry focus. If you are a consultant, then THAT ,in and of itself, is an industry and a core skill that will last through many hot software products. If, however, you have a heavy petroleum background, you might want to think twice about taking a permanent position on Burger King's SAP project, unless you want to make a permanent industry transition from petroleum to food service. If you do find yourself switching industries, just make sure this is an intentional choice with a long-term benefit. Using SAP as a roller coaster between different industries may not be good for your career, unless of course you see yourself as first and foremost a consultant. But in general, your technical skills will be more valuable if you pick one growing industry and focus on it.

This is all the more true since 1998, when SAP moved to an industry-focus for its sales and consulting. No longer can consultants remain generalists and surf from industry to industry. The product itself is becoming increasingly industry-specific as R/3 Version 4.0 can be broken into Retail Solutions, IS-OIL solutions, Automotive Solutions, and on and on.

Finally, it goes without saying that most R/2 experts should be plotting a transition to an R/3 environment. This is one area where you can use your SAP skills to make a very important switch. Indeed, many people have successfully used SAP to leverage themselves from a mainframe to a client/server background. With SAP's announcement that it will no longer support R/2 after 2004, the handwriting is on the wall in bold italics. The time is coming for you R/2 consultants to convert to R/3, either through delta training or by finding a position with a firm that will be moving from R/2 to R/3.

SAP Post Y2K

As for the underlying question to all of this…no one knows exactly what kind of future SAP has in the United States. Certainly demand for the SAP professional will continue at a high level through 2001 or 2002. Beyond that, much is riding on the success of the implementations currently underway. Equally important is SAP's ability to capture new markets and to continually expand the scope and functionality of R/3 beyond that of its competitors.

It is clear that 1999 and 2000 will be volatile and unpredictable years for ERP consultants on the whole. After year 2000, it is obvious that SAP will have to expand its market penetration into the so-called "extended ERP" market of supply chain, web-enabled applications in order to come close to maintaining the revenue growth of the preceding years. Now is as good a time as any to make some general assessments of the challenges SAP has overcome and the obstacles it will face in the coming years.

So how has SAP managed to survive and prosper despite the nay-sayers? Several factors have contributed to the longevity of the ERP market leader. First, the ongoing costs and hassles of integration have pushed clients away from a best of breed market. SAP is furthering its dominance in the core applications ERP market (FI, HR, basic manufacturing) through its strides in HR functionality, and it looks quite likely that SAP will continue to have success in FI, HR, and some basic manufacturing work across many industries. SAP has also managed to postpone its day of reckoning by maintaining a global, multi-currency presence and making great strides on industry-specific, targeted functionality.

Perhaps the greatest single accomplishment of SAP has been the successful development of the ASAP implementation methodology, and the resulting success in the mid-market. The ASAP methodology has provided a proven means of bringing implementations in, if not always on time, then certainly on a more timely basis. ASAP has also helped companies to identify the problem signs sooner, and as a result we see less of the ComputerWorld features on "SAP Implementations Gone Awry." The success in the mid-market has redefined R/3 somewhat from its historical roots as a tool of business process reengineering, provided by Big Five firms to Fortune 100 clients. In fact, Big Five firms are feeling the revenue squeeze, and it's clear that the health of SAP and the health of Big Five SAP consulting are two different questions entirely.

We think the Big Five will continue to capture a fair amount of the SAP business, although not from the mid-market, where these firms are not always wanted and where their interest in rolling up their sleeves has always been ambiguous. Many of the Big Five will end up finding new sources of traditional SAP consulting business by penetrating new vertical markets and drawing on expertise within the firm, much as KPMG is doing for SAP healthcare. SAP clients. However, not all of these new verticals are going to welcome SAP with open arms, and the dominance SAP has had in industries like consumer goods and aerospace may not translate as well to service industries and other hotly contested ERP markets.

Beyond Y2K, there may be another irony, as the Big Five will be amongst the first to capitalize on the extended SAP market, once the Fortune 100 clients who are already live on basic, core SAP modules install the new functionality. Someday the Big Five may once again dominate SAP consulting. Or not.

The end result is that SAP's success in the mid-market has bought it some time, but in the end, to stay ahead of the pack, more innovation will be necessary. Mid-market purse strings are tighter and the competition is intense. It is unrealistic to expect dominance in this area. It IS realistic to expect SAP to achieve real success in SAP HR functionality, and one of the most complicated things about being an SAP consultant in today's SAP market is that not all of the areas within SAP are paying the same right now; in fact, there is real disparity between different types of expertise.

We would rather predict the stock market than try to make an educated guess as to how SAP will fare in the midst of Y2K hysteria. Indeed, we even have the phenomenon of the "hesitant but very itchy finger," where clients ready to pull the trigger on big new projects seem hesitant to go forward until after 1999, even if they have already resolved their Y2K issues. The paranoia lingers.

Beyond Y2K, there are two schools of thought: one is that ERP markets will slow down as more large companies go live and everyone turns their attention to Internet commerce, supply chain optimization and even more supply chain optimization. The other school of thought is that ERP companies like SAP are in a good position to expand into these new areas, essentially extending the ERP functionality from within the boundaries of companies and out into the wild world of customers, vendors, and suppliers.

In our view, SAP is positioned to take advantage of some of this new business. It is clear that companies are much more likely to take a best-of-breed outlook in these areas that are so vital to external relationships, but as long as SAP can come close to the industry standard there should be a lot of business generated. This could create an additional five years or so of market-leading rates for SAP consultants who have managed to stay on the cutting edge of this new functionality.

After all, we are not talking about the end of SAP anytime in the next twenty years. All of us can look forward to rewarding careers in the field as long as the effort and skills are there. There is, however, a more burning question: will we see a time in the next few years where SAP consultants no longer set the bar for the "top dollar" rates? Will there come a time when supply chain implementation specialists, who implement suites that do not really even exist in a mature form at this time, will command more money than SAP professionals? It is entirely possible. But for those who do manage to follow SAP to the edge of the enterprise, we do believe you will find outstanding rates on the other side.

Two of the most important areas of SAP functionality currently "in the works" are the SAP Business Warehouse and the SCOPE/APO/Supply Chain Optimization initiative. There is also a sales force automation application underway in Walldorf. Of these three initiatives, Business Warehouse is the closest to being ready to storm the market, and there is a chance that some signature BW implementations will happen in the next six months. Beyond Y2K, the BW will be a very significant source of revenue growth for SAP. The question is, will companies balk at using SAP's own data warehousing tools or will they implement their own best-of-breed solution? We believe this is one area where SAP should do very well, and consultants who get involved with these initiatives should have some nice years ahead.

Best of all, it seems that both functional and technical folks will be in a position to be involved. On the functional side, SIS, LIS, SD, and CO-PA experts could get in on the BW action, and on the technical side, a fair amount of ABAPers and some select Basis people could add this to their toolkit nicely.

Obviously, SAP's SCOPE (supply chain optimization) package is going to be a major emphasis for SAP in the coming years. How successful it will be remains to be seen. Most analysts feel that SAP is about a year behind the best-of- breed solutions, which themselves are not fully realized. Some clients may balk at SAP trying to nudge into this area, others will leap at the chance to have fully integrated SAP supply chain and ERP installs.

It seems clear that APO, the advanced planning and scheduling portion of this product, should do very well, and create a new lease on life for SD/MM logistics consultants, who are naturally positioned to move into this new functionality as it develops. PP consultants might suffer the most, as APO functionality could well displace some of the already limited need for PP. We will be surprised if too much happens here before Y2K. Obviously, SAP's "learn (or some would say, 'borrow') from a partner and build it yourself" approach to new functionality is great for the integration burden but not so great in terms of getting new apps to market quickly.

No one can really know how these new initiatives will fare. But we are confident that the extended ERP market will breathe new life into the SAP market post-Y2K. The catch is to find a way to get involved. As for the "bread and butter" implementations, the demand will continue here too, although gradually leveling off a bit, with rates also gradually declining as a result, but still providing an important source of revenue for SAP and good positions for those who are comfortable in their current expertise.

Parting Words

One consultant we spoke to had a nice summary for how the SAP market has changed. Simply extend the following logic and you will have a slogan to follow if you wish for your career to flourish:

"A few years ago, all you had to do was have SAP on your resume, and you could get a job offer over the phone. Then companies started asking for functional or technical SAP experience, then they starting asking for configuration skills, then they asked for CO skills, then they asked for CO-PA skills, and now they ask for CO-PA skills in a retail environment."

Next they will ask for CO-PA skills in the clothing retail environment and knowledge of stitch machine interfaces will be a plus.

In the end, the only approach that is guaranteed is a basic one: continual skills improvement, and a fierce commitment to staying on top of where SAP is going.

Addendum: Taken from the *SAP Blue Book, A Concise Business Guide to the World of SAP.*

Apologia: for those of you who have already read this book, we apologize for being redundant. What follows is an edited excerpt which we feel will prove cautionary for all SAP consultants who seek to have a long-lasting career.

When SAP is $AP

The exploding SAP market and the consequent massive shortfall of experienced R/3 consultants have given rise to an unhealthy subculture, driven largely by greed, which makes it difficult for clients to sort through their consulting options. These are some of the highjinks you run into on a weekly basis when swimming the often murky SAP consulting waters:

Bait and switch: A firm bidding to become a client's implementation partner promotes star consultants during the proposal phase and sends inferior consultants once the deal is set.

Flooding the zone: A firm assigns one or two star consultants to a project and surrounds them with an army of neophyte consultants whose SAP experience can be measured in weeks. It takes a while for the client to recognize this because at the onset of a project, neophytes *seem* to know so much more than the client, but mostly they are hiding behind a terminology smoke-screen.

Gin rummy (spades) : A haves-and-needs body shopper sends a subcontract consultant to a client; some time later, the body shopper finds a cheaper consultant for the same job and, through some pretext, replaces the first one for greater personal profit. Gin rummy (clubs): A contract consultant accepts a six-month assignment. Two months into the job, the consultant finds another assignment that pays more. Citing 'philosophical differences', he/she abandons the first client in mid-project.

Casper Consulting, Inc.: Resumes of non-existent consultants are presented to clients to puff up the size of a consulting roster. Not so curiously, these consultants are always 'on another assignment'.

Sap, not SAP: Resumes are sprinkled with SAP initials like SD, MM, or PP but the candidate has no real SAP experience. This gambit is widespread since anyone who can fake their way into a job will get the requisite experience toward making the resume true. A candidate once called us and opened his spiel by saying that he had three years of *sap* experience. That's what he said, sap (rhymes with zap), not SAP. He means to put the moves on me and he cannot even pronounce it correctly? Imagine the resonance of a phone slamming onto its receiver.

Facing Mirrors(((()))): There are great numbers of contract consultants who cut subcontract representation deals with more than one consulting firm and thus appear on several firms' rosters. These consultants are only slightly more available than those from Casper Consulting, Inc.

In past years, consultant jokes have begun to replace lawyer jokes, which signifies the general public's mistrust and occasional loathing of all consultants. Because of the high dollar aspect of SAP, such consultants often inspire more than their usual share. The bad behavior listed above only contributes to a degradation of confidence in SAP consultants and reflects badly (and unfairly) on SAP itself.

Given previous shortfalls in the SAP consulting ranks, much of this behavior was tolerated from 1993 through 1997. This is no longer the case and the world of SAP is still just small enough that those consultants and body shoppers who play these games are known and increasingly shunned.

Reference Shelf

Glossary of Terms

About the Authors

How to Get the Latest SAP Career Information

A Final Word to Readers from Jon Reed, 2004

Glossary of Terms

ABAP/4	Advanced Business Application Programming Language (4th level)
AM	Fixed Assets Management application in SAP
ASAP	the Accelerated SAP method for implementing SAP R/3
AS-IS	a study of current ways of working, culminating in charts and scripts to be thrown away. Usually precedes a TO BE phase
Basis	The middleware that manages client/server functions across R/3
BEW	Business Engineering Workbench
Business Process	a group or series of activities by which inputs are turned to outputs that benefit the customer
C/S	Client/server
CBS	Certified Business Solutions (SAP program for small firms)
CO	Controlling application in SAP R/3
Configure	filling in R/3 tables (and appropriate combinations) to make the software work as desired
Customize	Effect changes to SAP software so it will fit your process designs
FI	Financial application in SAP R/3
Gap analysis	What you want less what R/3 can do for you = gap analysis (usually off the mark)
GUI	Graphical User Interface
HR	Human Resources application in SAP R/3
ICOE	Industry Centers of Expertise (e.g. Oil & Gas, Automotive, Health Care)
Interfaces	Program-driven connections between disparate data bases
IS	Information systems
IS	Industry Solutions application in SAP
IT	Information technology

Middleware (Basis)	The / between client and server, as in Client/Server
MM	Materials management application in R/3
PM	Production Maintenance application in SAP R/3
Portability	the capacity of software to run on operating systems from disparate platform suppliers
PP	Production Planning application in SAP R/3
PS	Project System application in SAP R/3
QA	Quality Assurance in SAP R/3
QM	Quality Management application in SAP R/3
SAP	Pronounced Ess Ay Pee; the supplier
SD	Sales and distribution application in SAP R/3
Software suite	Multiple software applications derived from common design
TO BE	the charting and scripting of new business processes

About the Authors

Jon Reed is the Director of Online Content for mySAPcareers.com. He is also the SAP Career Expert for SearchSAP.com's "Ask the Expert" panel. Jon is the author of the "SAP eCareer Transitions Newsletter," a weekly email newsletter for SAP professionals who are moving into new areas of the mySAP product line. Since 2003, Jon has also served as the Managing Editor of SAPtips (www.SAPtips.com), a leading publication on technical and functional SAP project know-how.

Over the years, through his newsletters and personal consultations, Jon Reed has advised thousands of SAP professionals on their job searches and project choices. Jon believes that the key to long-term success in SAP is to develop a career strategy that parallels SAP's own evolution from "back-end" solution to "outward-facing" e-business architecture. Jon can be reached by email at jon.sap@verizon.net.

Michael Doane is a senior consultant specializing in SAP management and education. He has twenty-five years of business systems experience in the U.S., Europe, and Asia and has lectured widely about SAP to executives.

He is the author of *In the Path of the Whirlwind, An Apprentice Guide to the World of SAP* and *Capturing the Whirlwind, Your Field Guide to a Successful SAP Implementation* as well as the recent *SAP Blue Book, A Concise Business Guide to the World of SAP*. He can be reached via e-mail at micdoane@aol.com.

Thanks to Our Contributors:

Michael and Jon would like to extend a heartfelt thanks to the contributors to the original '99 edition of the *SAP Consultant Handbook*: Betty Costa, Patti Walsh, Scott Gilbert, Michael West, George Zatulovsky, and Rob Doane. Thanks for devoting your expertise and helping this book to become the industry standard.

How to Get the Latest SAP Market Information

New SAP Consulting and Market Information:
How to Get Jon Reed's Latest SAP Career Advice

Jon Reed regularly publishes updated SAP consulting and career information, much of it with readers of this book in mind. Here are the web sites where you can go and gain access to this content:

www.mySAPcareers.com

Hosted by eCommQuest and run by Jon Reed, mySAPcareers.com is a free online resource for independent SAP consultants. The purpose of mySAPcareers.com is to provide career information that supports the SAP consultant in transition. In the site's career archives, Jon features in-depth interviews with expert SAP consultants who have broken into emerging areas of SAP and mySAP such as Portals, SEM, and BW. Jon also does annual "hot SAP skills" market projections, and there are a number of articles and interviews that address ways that SAP consultants are responding to offshore outsourcing. Jon's "mySAP Quarterly Reviews" provide in-depth analysis of the most important SAP news stories of the year. eCommQuest, the staffing firm that hosts mySAPcareers.com, is an SAP and e-Business staffing firm, and site visitors can browse through eCommQuest's latest SAP positions as well as the in-depth career content.

---

www.SearchSAP.com

In his "Ask the Expert" career column, Jon provides detailed answers to the latest SAP career concerns, from surviving outsourcing and the future of ABAP, to the unfolding opportunities in NetWeaver, mySAP CRM, Enterprise Portals, SAP Java Development, etc.

You can see almost two years of archived career questions by logging on to SearchSAP.com and clicking on the blue "Experts" tab on the blue horizontal menu bar.

Jon also answers SAP career questions live on the first Tuesday of each month, from 12 to 3pm eastern time, in the SearchSAP discussion forum. You can find that forum by logging onto SearchSAP.com, and clicking on "discussions" on the left hand menu bar. There is a year and a half of archived questions and answers from the discussion to read as well. Note that you may have to register with SearchSAP (free) to post questions to the forum.

---

www.SAPtips.com

Jon serves as the Managing Editor of SAPtips (www.SAPtips.com), a popular SAP implementation publication authored by expert SAP consultants who provide honest, project-based insights on "what works and what doesn't" across the SAP product line. SAPtips covers the entire range of the SAP and mySAP product line on both the functional and technical side. SAPtips is an online, subscription-based publication, but you can obtain free sample white papers and sample editions of the *SAPtips Journal* by logging onto the SAPtips.com web site. In the reviews and previews section, you can also read all of the letters to readers Jon has written for SAPtips since it began.

If you like reading honest, opinionated, expert advice on SAP project management and hands-on SAP techniques, you'll want to check out SAPtips.

Special deal for *SAP Consultant Handbook* readers: for a limited time, any SAP professional who has purchased this book and who writes a detailed review of a sample edition of SAPtips is eligible for a one year free subscription to SAPtips. For more details, email Jon Reed at jon.sap@verizon.net. Jon views SAPtips as his culminating achievement in the SAP market, and encourages you to give it a close look.

---

www.SAPGenie.com

Jon Reed is now authoring a quarterly opinion column for SAPGenie.com, entitled "SAP Career Outlook." Each column tackles a hot button issue for SAP professionals and consultants, and makes skills recommendations based on the latest market trends. The first article, entitled "A Hard Look At SAP Outsourcing: How Much Has it Hurt Consultants, and What Can Be Done About It?" is a hard-hitting and personal take on the impact of SAP outsourcing. For this column (and more) of the same, go to SAPGenie.com, and scroll down the right hand side of the home page menu until you hit the "SAP Scoop" link promoting the column. Note that you can also view sample articles from SAPtips on SAPGenie.com by following the link right above the "SAP Scoop" link on the right hand column of the home page.

A Closing Word from Jon Reed:

I hope you've enjoyed the *SAP Consultant Handbook*, and that it has helped you solidify your approach to achieving success in SAP consulting. I have heard from numerous readers who have taken their SAP careers to the next level (and avoided costly downtime) by applying the methodologies outlined in this book.

I do expect the SAP consulting market to continue to evolve, and I plan to eventually write a companion volume to this book that details the keys to successful SAP consulting in the NetWeaver era. But in the meantime, I suggest you follow a two-pronged approach that other readers of this book have used effectively:

1. Use this book to gain a clear sense of the history of the SAP consulting market and how it has evolved, with a particular eye towards the "career best practices" that are timeless.

2. Update your SAP market knowledge through a continued commitment to self-education. A great place to start is with the free and sample materials I've detailed in the last few pages, since much of it was put together with readers of this book in mind.

Good luck in your SAP career!

Jon Reed
Vice President and Managing Editor, SAPtips.com

CAREER PLAN

1. FICO ; Implementation + ofety/Controlling
   Business Process Expérieu
   ie. (functional)

2. HR → pfT course @ FRS School

3. Authorizations.

4. Project Management.

5. NetWeaver + other SAP Technology
   y. Business Objects.

6. Industry focus. eg Retail; Oil, utilitie

7. Speak to people with Industry exp.
   and SAP Implementation exp.
   it chages y. MR India.

Printed in the United Kingdom
by Lightning Source UK Ltd.
129727UK00001B/84/A

9 780972 598804